The Complete Guide to
TOOLS AND MATERIALS

This book is dedicated to my wife Jean, who is
wallpapering as I sit at my typewriter.

Grateful thanks also to Stephen Bull
for his invaluable help.

The Complete Guide to
TOOLS AND MATERIALS

For Everyone from the Beginner to
the DIY Enthusiast and Professional

Written and illustrated by
Arthur Baker

BCA
LONDON · NEW YORK · SYDNEY · TORONTO

This edition published in 1992
by BCA by arrangement with
Collins & Brown Ltd
Mercury House
195 Knightsbridge
London SW7 1RE

A CIP catalogue record for this book is available from the
British Library

CN 2443

Editorial Director: Gabrielle Townsend
Editor: Colin Ziegler
Art Director: Roger Bristow

Typeset by August Filmsetting, Haydock, St Helens
Printed in Great Britain by Clays Ltd, Bungay

CONTENTS

Introduction

Designed as a detailed reference book for use by all householders—from complete novices to experienced DIYers—this book will show you not only what tools are applicable to certain jobs but also what materials and manufactured items are used on such jobs. You will find information that will apply to your particular needs by looking at the contents list or the index.

It will not show you how to do the various decorating jobs. There is a large range of instructional books on sale or they can be borrowed from your local library. You should refer to one of these particularly if you are working on electrical or plumbing jobs.

You will find this book a very useful reference, however, for almost any job that a householder is likely to tackle. For example; laying a concrete base for a garden shed? Turn to page 99 and you will find the mix required, the recommended thickness for a shed including the type and thickness for the sub-base and also how to calculate the number of bags of cement and the quantity of ballast—so avoiding ordering too little or too much. Even unopened cement does not keep well and that pile of sand lying in the drive for months can be an eyesore.

By the very nature of the DIY market, products come and go, so I have tried to avoid including the more esoteric offerings but even so, some of the items listed will disappear from the shelves to be replaced by others.

Make full use of the DIY superstores when planning any big job. Quite often they have free leaflets available to cover certain projects. Collect colour cards when redecorating. These are always useful to study at home and compare with existing furnishings.

Planning

The good design that you admire in a book or magazine is not just the result of a happy accident. Interior designers spend time agonizing over colour, pattern and form of all the elements that go to make an attractive and functional room setting.

It will pay you not to rush into a new decorating project, but to study carefully what you want. A bit of extra care and patience at this stage will pay dividends later. Never rush a decorating job. Plan well ahead. Preparation is the key to a satisfying and long-lasting decoration job. For example, painting over old, peeling paint is an utter waste of time.

Decorating a room

Order of work

1. Collect decorating ideas from books, magazines and by studying displays in stores or even room settings on television. Make notes of paint, wallpaper, carpets, curtains and blinds. Compare paint colours with wallpapers, carpets and curtains. Note prices.
2. Measure relevant areas for decorating; wallpaper or ceiling paper areas, large paint areas, windows. For estimating wallpaper requirements see page 10. For paint types and coverage see pages 14–17.
3. Check for any structural alterations that may be needed—extra sockets, curing damp, replastering areas of walls—note your specific requirements and refer to the appropriate section of this book.
4. Make a shopping list. Ensure that you have the relevant tools as well as the materials for the preparation of areas to be redecorated.
5. Starting work: Remove lampshades,

pictures, loose shelving, curtains or blinds and floor coverings. Fitted carpets need to be removed if you are painting skirting boards. If not, cover with strong plastic sheeting taped into place with heavy duty masking tape. Cover this with old dust sheets as plastic sheeting can be slippery. Repair any tears as soon as they occur. Dried emulsion paint is impossible to remove from carpets! If fitted carpets are to be removed and re-laid arrange to have this done professionally.
6. It's often difficult in a cramped family house to empty the room completely. Temporary storage may be possible in your garage. If there is no alternative storage available then at least move the furniture to the centre of the room and cover it with inexpensive dust sheets available from DIY stores.

Note. Carpet-layers will insist on an empty room before they will start work.

7. Remove wallpaper and ceiling paper either with a wallpaper steamer (see page 11) or by soaking and scraping. A pump-up garden sprayer is excellent for soaking wallpaper.
8. Remove old gloss paint on wood by hot-air gun or chemical stripper (see page 13), or if it is in good condition rub down and clean.
9. Thoroughly rub down and clean all surfaces and wash with warm water and sugar soap or a proprietary cleaner (see page 16).
10. Complete all structural improvements. Refer to relevant sections.
11. Check wooden floors for woodworm or fungus attack (see page 82). Screw down loose or creaking floorboards. If sanding floorboards for a decorative finish, hire the necessary equipment and do this next.
12. Fill all holes and cracks in plaster and

wood, allow to dry overnight (longer for large or deep plaster repairs) and rub down flat.

13. Vacuum the whole room carefully then wipe all the woodwork with a cloth dampened with white spirit (or use a tack rag).

14. Knot and prime bare areas of wood (see page 16) and leave overnight to dry.

15. Undercoat all woodwork. Leave overnight.

16. Lightly sand undercoated woodwork and wipe clean. If bare plaster is to be painted this can be done before topcoating woodwork.

17. Topcoat all woodwork. Leave overnight to dry.

18. Size walls and ceilings if these are to be papered (see page 10).

19. Paper ceilings and walls. If the wallpaper or ceiling paper is to be painted allow the paper to dry overnight before painting.

20. Clean up and retouch any missed areas. Remove protective covers and vacuum the room thoroughly. Clean the windows and sills and any radiators. Stand back and admire.

Summary

1. Collect info.
2. Measure up.
3. Plan structural changes.
4. Make shopping list. Buy materials.
5. Clear room.
6. Cover non-removable items.
7. Strip wallpaper.
8. Prepare paintwork.
9. Sand down.
10. Complete structural work.
11. Check for woodworm etc.
12. Fill damaged areas.

13. Clean, prior to painting.
14. Prime wood.
15. Undercoat wood.
16. Sand wood. Paint plaster.
17. Topcoat all woodwork.
18. Size walls for papering.
19. Paper ceilings and walls.
20. Clean up.

Provisional list of tools and materials

Notepad
Colour charts
Dust sheets
Masking tape
Sandpaper (various grades)
White spirit or brush cleaner
Tack rags
Filler
Clean tins for brush cleaning
Wallpaper paste
Paints: knotting / primer / undercoat / gloss / emulsion
Tools:
Expanding rule
Bucket and sponge
Scraper or filling knife
Sanding block
Spot board (smooth piece of hardboard for mixing filler)
Paint brushes (small for gloss, large for emulsion)
Paste brush
Wallpaper brush
Plumb line or builder's level
Steel straightedge and craft knife (for cutting wallpaper)
Paperhanger's scissors

Optional equipment to hire:
Wallpaper stripper
Floorboard sander

Safety in the home

Statistics show that the home is quite a hazardous place to be. Factories and offices are closely monitored by the Health and Safety Inspectorate but no such safety net exists for the home. You must be your own health and safety inspector.

Using tools and materials safely

Using tools and materials safely

Always keep tools sharp. A blunt tool requires much more force to cut and is therefore more dangerous to use. Invest in a good oilstone (see page 38) and use it often.

Put tools away as soon as you've finished with them especially when there are young children in the house. With cutting tools always keep the hands behind the cutting edge and work away from the body.

When cutting or drilling concrete or masonry always wear safety goggles. In fact it makes good sense to wear them whenever using power tools of any sort. When drilling or machine sawing dusty materials or power sanding wear a dust mask.

When using noisy equipment such as pneumatic hammers wear ear defenders as well.

Wear heavy duty gloves when handling hardcore, as freshly broken concrete exposes shattered flints and these produce minute cuts and make the fingertips very sore. Handle wet cement as little as possible as the lime can irritate the skin.

Basic toolkit

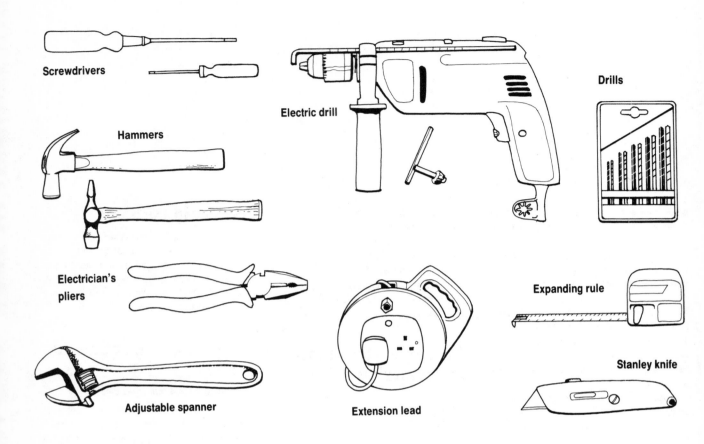

Screwdrivers

Hammers

Electric drill

Drills

Electrician's pliers

Adjustable spanner

Extension lead

Expanding rule

Stanley knife

The basic household toolkit

Throughout this book you will find constant reference to tools which are required to do this or that job. To kit yourself out with all these tools you would need a second mortgage. These are there mainly to show how a tool designed for a specific purpose and often evolved over many decades can make that particular job easier and more satisfying. Most tools are acquired over a lifetime of tackling different jobs; but also remember to study the list of local tool-hire shops to see what you can hire for short periods.

When you move into your own home for the first time you will need certain basic tools just to keep things running and avoid being dependent on other people. The following is a list of tools which should be acquired as soon as is practical. You can find more detailed information throughout the book.

Screwdrivers

Buy several. A small slim-bladed one is essential for electric plugs and terminals. A medium slot and medium cross-head should cover immediate needs. Page 75.

Hammer

Cross-pein or claw. A claw hammer is useful for pulling nails out but a cross-pein makes a better general purpose tool. The pein is used for starting nails. Page 73.

Electrician's pliers

These are useful for all sorts of jobs as well as any wiring work. Page 51.

Adjustable spanner

Get one with a jaw opening of 35 mm ($1\frac{3}{8}$ in). You will find it invaluable. Page 43.

Electric drill

The only expensive item on this list. Buy one with a hammer action. This is a necessity even if you only want to hang a picture or put up shelves. You will, at some time or other, need to drill into masonry and an electric hammer drill is the only practical way to do this. Page 46.

Extension lead

One of about 6 metres (20 ft) with two outlets and a built-in overload device is ideal for your electric drill and other household appliances.

Drills

Mixed set of HSS twist and masonry drills. A handy set would range from 1.5 mm to 6 mm ($\frac{1}{16}$ to $\frac{1}{4}$ in) and cover most wall plug sizes. Page 37.

Expanding rule

One marked in both metric and imperial sizes and about 3.5 m (12 ft) long is useful about the house.

Stanley knife

With easily replaceable blades this is useful for cutting vinyl, cork, card and paper.

Basic toolkit

Spirit level

Stepladder

Torch

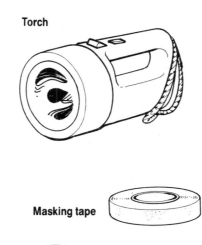

Masking tape

Cellulose thinners

Household oil

Spirit level

A small handy level will ensure that your shelves are perfectly horizontal.

Stepladders

Indispensable for general household cleaning and maintenance as well as any decorating work. Page 90.

Torch

One of the most essential items for any home. If anything goes wrong, inside or out, it will be on a dark winter's night. Check often to see that the batteries are still good.

Masking tape

A roll of 25 mm (1 in) wide masking tape has an infinite variety of uses. Low-tack adhesive means it's easy to remove after use. Uses include tidying coiled cables, marking delicate surfaces on which you don't wish to write, wrapping around twist drills to indicate depths (if you leave a flag sticking out it even blows away sawdust for better visiblity), writing temporary instructions on smooth surfaces and sticking up notes in the workshop. All this as well as its intended purpose of masking paintwork.

Cellulose thinners

Buy a small tin (250 ml) of this at your local auto accessory shop. It's a very good cleaning agent and evaporates rapidly. It's the only solvent I have found which will remove the residue of those little sticky labels that suppliers attach to everything from toilet pans to timber.

Warning. Cellulose thinners are highly inflammable and give off strong fumes. They may harm some plastics—check on a hidden area first.

Household oil

A small tin of light household oil will ease all sorts of problems throughout the house.

Wallpaper

Wallpaper types

Standard wallpaper

Printed papers in various weights

Relief wallpapers

Heavily embossed papers in heavyweight paper for over painting.

Woodchip papers

Heavyweight paper with woodchips embossed into it during manufacture. For over painting.

Special effect relief wallpapers

Available as imitation brick, stone, wood panelling, etc.

Vinyls

Smooth vinyl

Thin PVC bonded to a backing paper. Hard-wearing and easy to clean.

Ready pasted vinyl

The adhesive-coated backing removes the need to paste. The cut length is soaked in a water trough and then hung.

Embossed vinyl

Moulded PVC on a strong backing paper.

Blown vinyl

PVC is expanded during manufacture to produce a lightweight heavily embossed pattern with a flat backing.

Foamed polyethylene (Novamura)

This wallcovering has a soft fabric feel. Apply paste to the wall instead of the paper.

Relief vinyl

Photographic and moulded reproductions of various materials: brick, stone, timber panelling and ceramic tiles.

Wallpaper pastes

Various types of wallpaper paste are available to suit different wallpaper types. Refer to the wallpaper pack to see what the manufacturer recommends, or look at the paste pack for guidance.

General purpose cellulose pastes in powder form can be used in different mixes to suit different weights of paper. A fungicidal paste must be used with vinyls and washable papers to avoid mould forming on the wall under the paper.

Overlap and border adhesive

With the increasing popularity of borders and friezes, a special border and overlap adhesive is now available in large tubes. This will even stick vinyl to vinyl, previously a problem area.

Wallpaper estimating chart

Height from top of skirting board to ceiling or picture rail in metres	Distance around the room in metres (include windows and doors)											Height from top of skirting board to ceiling or picture rail in feet
	10	11	12	13	14	15	16	17	18	19	20	
1.83 – 2.15	5	5	5	6	6	7	7	7	8	8	9	6'0"–7'0"
2.15 – 2.30	5	5	6	6	7	7	7	8	8	9	9	7'0"–7'6"
2.30 – 2.45	5	6	6	7	7	7	8	8	9	9	10	7'6"–8'0"
2.45 – 2.60	5	6	6	7	7	8	8	9	9	10	10	8'0"–8'6"
2.60 – 2.75	6	6	7	7	8	8	9	9	10	10	11	8'6"–9'0"
2.75 – 2.90	6	7	7	8	8	9	9	10	10	11	11	9'0"–9'6"
2.90 – 3.00	6	7	7	8	8	9	10	10	11	11	12	9'6"–10'0"
	33	36	39	43	46	49	52	56	59	62	66	
	Distance around the room in feet (include windows and doors)											

If you wish to make your own calculations, use this formula: measure the total distance around the room ignoring doors and windows unless these are exceptionally large. Multiply this figure by the height of the wall—floor to ceiling or floor to picture rail—to give the total papering area.

Multiply the length of the wallpaper roll (usually 10 m [33 ft]) by the width of the roll (usually 0.53 m [21 in]) to give the total area of the wallpaper roll, 0.53 m × 10 m (21 in × 33 ft) = 5.30 m² (57 sq ft). Divide this figure into the total wall area to give the number of rolls required.

Measuring ceilings

Divide the area of the roll into the area of the ceiling to give the number of rolls required.

Drop pattern wallpapers

Buy extra rolls where a large pattern repeats down a sheet. Shops will normally take back unopened rolls if you over order.

Soaking time

When pasting wallpapers, each sheet should be allowed the same time to soak after pasting to equalize the expansion of the paper. A length of pasted paper can gain 25 mm (1 in) and make pattern matching difficult. Allow three to four minutes for medium-weight papers and up to ten minutes for heavyweights.

Tools

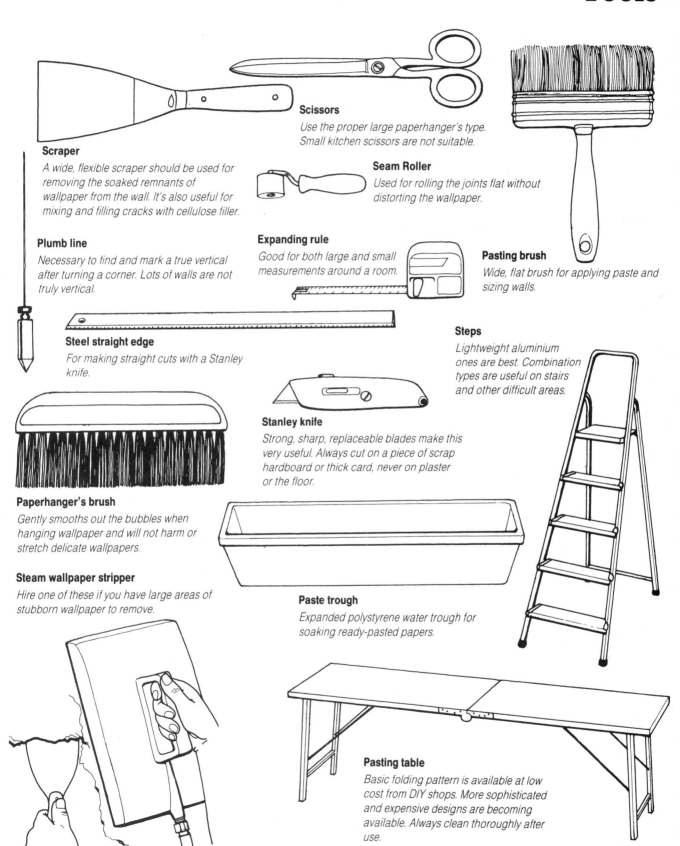

Scissors

Use the proper large paperhanger's type. Small kitchen scissors are not suitable.

Scraper

A wide, flexible scraper should be used for removing the soaked remnants of wallpaper from the wall. It's also useful for mixing and filling cracks with cellulose filler.

Seam Roller

Used for rolling the joints flat without distorting the wallpaper.

Plumb line

Necessary to find and mark a true vertical after turning a corner. Lots of walls are not truly vertical.

Expanding rule

Good for both large and small measurements around a room.

Pasting brush

Wide, flat brush for applying paste and sizing walls.

Steel straight edge

For making straight cuts with a Stanley knife.

Steps

Lightweight aluminium ones are best. Combination types are useful on stairs and other difficult areas.

Stanley knife

Strong, sharp, replaceable blades make this very useful. Always cut on a piece of scrap hardboard or thick card, never on plaster or the floor.

Paperhanger's brush

Gently smooths out the bubbles when hanging wallpaper and will not harm or stretch delicate wallpapers.

Steam wallpaper stripper

Hire one of these if you have large areas of stubborn wallpaper to remove.

Paste trough

Expanded polystyrene water trough for soaking ready-pasted papers.

Pasting table

Basic folding pattern is available at low cost from DIY shops. More sophisticated and expensive designs are becoming available. Always clean thoroughly after use.

Brushes

Good quality bristle brushes are essential for obtaining a good paint finish. Clean them immediately after use with the proper solvent.

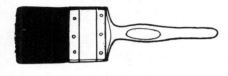

Flat lining tool

For painting edges and corners.

Flat brushes

Use smaller sizes for gloss and larger sizes for emulsion. Available in the following sizes:
12 mm ($\frac{1}{2}$ in.), 20 mm ($\frac{3}{4}$ in.), 25 mm (1 in.), 38 mm ($1\frac{1}{2}$ in.), 50 mm (2 in.), 64 mm ($2\frac{1}{2}$ in.), 75 mm (3 in.), 100 mm (4 in.) and 125 mm (5 in.).

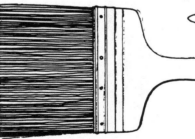

Distemper brushes

Wide, flat brushes in a range of sizes for covering large areas quickly. Also useful as wallpaper pasting brushes.

Radiator brush

Used to get at awkward areas like the backs of radiators. There is also a slim, long-handled roller for the same purpose.

Textured paint finishes

Using the new textured paint and one of the various patterned applicators, such as comb, stipple brush or special rollers, all sorts of patterns can be made with the paint.

Patterned rollers

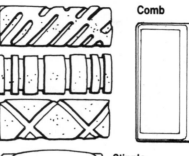

Comb

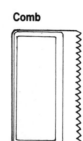

Stipple brush

Use a paint tray to load rollers.

Tar brush

Disposable brush for applying bitumen to roofs.

Paint kettle

Paint container that is useful when working up ladders, etc.

Paint pads

Flat pads with mohair painting surfaces. Available in sizes from 38 mm ($1\frac{1}{2}$ in.) to 152 mm (6 in.) wide.

Paint roller

Rollers are made from foam, lambswool and mohair.

Tip

To stop paint brush bristles from splaying out when painting up to glass on window frames, wrap masking tape around the bristles.

Preparation

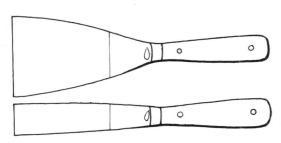

Scrapers

Use with a hot-air gun, blowtorch or chemical stripper for removing softened paint.

Wire brush

For removing rust and loose flaking paint from metal.

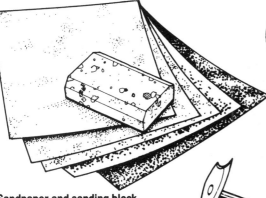

Sandpaper and sanding block

Use a cork sandpaper block to stop the abrasive overheating and clogging with paint.

Abrasive paper

Abrasive papers are made in a variety of grits. Glasspaper is cheap, but wears quickly. Garnet paper is more expensive, but is superb for fine woodwork. Aluminium oxide is very hard and.is freely available in sheets for power sanders. Silicon carbide is used mainly wet for metal finishing.

The standard sheet size of abrasive papers is 230 mm (9 in.) by 280 mm (11 in.), although other sizes are available specifically for machine sanders.

The grading of abrasive papers varies between manufacturers, but five basic grades are available: very coarse, coarse, medium, fine and very fine.

Wire brushes

Two types, cup and disc, can be mounted in an electric drill and are very effective at removing rust and paint from intricate metal shapes. Always wear eye protection.

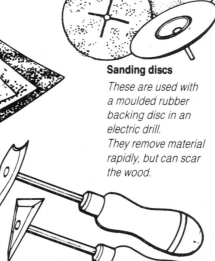

Sanding discs

These are used with a moulded rubber backing disc in an electric drill. They remove material rapidly, but can scar the wood.

Shave hooks

Triangular and curved. Very useful for getting into intricate mouldings.

Drum sander

A circular foam-plastic block with a band of renewable abrasive paper. For use in an electric drill.

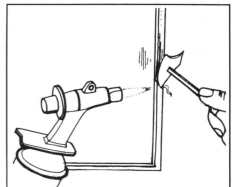

Gas blowtorches will soften old oil paint quickly, but need to be used with care where inflammable materials are present. Heat is not so effective on old emulsion paint.

Electric hot-air guns are safer, but will still scorch wood if used indiscriminately, particularly around mouldings.

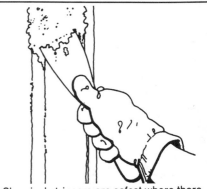

Chemical strippers are safest where there is danger of fire or if you wish to strip back old woodwork and coat with a clear finish. Ventilate the room well when using chemical strippers and wear rubber gloves.

Paint

Basically, there are two types of paint used in home decoration — water-based emulsions for plaster, papered walls and ceilings, and oil-based paints for wood and metal surfaces. Emulsions should never be used on bare metal as it will stain.

Type	Inside or out	Use	Application
Water-based:			
Emulsion, vinyl silk	Interior	Plaster, papered surfaces, wood,	Brush/Roller/Pad
Emulsion, vinyl matt	Interior	expanded polystyrene tiles and	Brush/Roller/Pad
Emulsion, solid	Interior	coving	Roller
Emulsion, one-coat	Interior	As above	Brush/Roller/Pad
Emulsion, machine-mixed in store	Interior	As above	Brush/Roller/Pad
Acrylic wood primer	Interior/Exterior	Clean bare wood	Brush
Oil-based:			
Liquid gloss	Interior/Exterior	Wood, metal, plastic, putty	Brush/Roller/Pad
Non-drip gloss	Interior/Exterior	Wood, metal, plastic, putty	Brush/Roller/Pad
One-coat gloss	Interior/Exterior	Wood, metal, plastic, putty	Brush/Roller/Pad
Flexible wood gloss	Exterior	Wood only	Brush
Undercoat	Interior/Exterior	Wood, metal, plastic, putty	Brush
Primer, wood	Interior/Exterior	Wood, plastic, putty	Brush
Primer, metal	Interior/Exterior	Metal only	Brush
Clear wood varnish:			
Acrylic varnish	Interior	Hardwood and softwood	Brush/Pad
Non-drip varnish	Interior/Exterior	Hardwood and softwood	Brush/Pad
Polyurethane varnish	Interior/Exterior	Hardwood and softwood	Brush/Pad
Floor and cork varnish	Interior	Cork tiles, wooden flooring	Brush
Yacht varnish	Interior/Exterior	Hardwood and softwood	Brush
Stains:			
Wood dye	Interior/Exterior	Hardwood and softwood	Brush/Cloth pad
Wood lightener	Interior/Exterior	Hardwood and softwood	Brush/Steel wool
Tinted wood varnish:			
Wood-toned varnish	Interior/Exterior	Hardwood and softwood	Brush/Pad
Coloured wood varnish	Interior	Hardwood and softwood	Brush/Pad
Specialized exterior finishes:			
Preservative primer	Exterior	Wood	Brush
Aluminium wood primer	Exterior	Resinous wood	Brush
Exterior undercoat	Exterior	Wood	Brush
Wood sealer	Exterior	Bare wood	Brush
Stabilizing solution	Interior/Exterior	Old brickwork and rendering	Brush
Emulsion-based masonry paint	Exterior	Concrete, stone, brick	Brush
Cement-based masonry paint	Exterior	Concrete, stone, brick	Brush
Doorstep paint	Interior/Exterior	Concrete, stone, brick, unglazed tiles	Brush
Matt roof-tile paint	Exterior	Roof tiles, brick, masonry	Brush
Bitumen waterpoof seal	Exterior	Felt roofs, flashings, gutters	Brush
Bitumen metal paint	Exterior	Exterior metal, asbestos sheet	Brush
Bitumen crack filler	Exterior	Felt roofs, flashings, gutters	Trowel
Special purpose paints:			
Damp sealer	Interior/Exterior	Plaster and brick	Brush
Stain sealer	Interior	Plaster and brick	Brush
Floor paint	Interior	Concrete, stone, paving, lino, wood	Brush
Concrete floor sealer	Interior	Concrete	Brush
Textured wall paint	Interior/Exterior	Powder mix, make-your-own patterns	Brush, initially

Paint

*Coverage depends on the surfaces and is for rough guidance only.

Properties	Coverage* (per litre)	Brush cleaner/Thinner	Colour range
Smooth-flowing, opaque. Dries to a slight sheen. Washable.	12 m²	Water	Brilliant white and pale colours
As above. Dries matt.	12 m²	Water	Brilliant white and pale colours
Non-drip. Formulated for ceilings.	12 m²	Water	Brilliant white and pale colours
Especially high opacity.	8 m²	Water	Brilliant white and pale colours
Excellent for colour matching.	12 m²	Water	Vast range of colours
Easy to use, quick-drying wood primer.	12 m²	Water	White and grey
Tough, durable, weather-resistant high-gloss finish.	17 m²	White spirit	Bright colours
Thixotropic. As above.	12 m²	White spirit	Bright colours
Self-undercoating gloss finish.	12 m²	White spirit	Bright colours
Flexible finish. Moves with the wood.	17 m²	White spirit	Bright colours
Thick, filling coat. Finish with gloss.	16 m²	White spirit	Special undercoat colours
Seals the pores of the wood. Use with undercoat/gloss.	5–12 m²	White spirit	White and pink
Prepares bare metal for finishing coats.	12 m²	White spirit	White and grey
Easy to use, quick-drying varnish.	16 m²	Water	Clear
Thicker, clear varnish.	16 m²	White spirit	Clear
Hard finish. Available in gloss or satin.	16 m²	White spirit	Clear
Hardwearing finish. Seals and protects cork from staining.	10 m²	Water	Clear
Highly weather-resistant, clear finish.	10 m²	White spirit	Clear
For staining both hardwoods and softwoods.	36 m²	See pack	Hardwood colours
Bleaches certain woods. Check pack for details.	—	See pack	—
Varnish and stain in one operation.	20 m²	White spirit	Hardwood colours
Transparent colours which still show the wood grain.	20 m²	White spirit	Pale transparent hues
Wood primer containing preservative for outside use.	20 m²	White spirit	White and pink
For oily woods and knots.	12 m²	White spirit	White
Specifically for wood in exposed situations.	10 m²	White spirit	White
Seals exterior wood against moisture.	20 m²	White spirit	Clear
Seals old, dusty walls prior to painting.	12 m²	White spirit	Clear
Easy-to-use exterior masonry paint.	10 m²	Water	Brilliant white and pale colours
Contains cement for extra weather resistance.	9 m²	Water	Brilliant white and pale colours
High gloss, non-slip step paint.	10 m²	White spirit	Red
Protective and decorative finish for roof tiles.	7 m²	White spirit	Red
Protects and waterproofs roofing materials.	10 m²	White spirit	Black
Protective finish for gutters, railings, etc.	12 m²	White spirit	Black
Thick mastic for sealing exterior cracks.	—	White spirit	Black
Stops penetrating damp. Overpaint or paper after use.	11 m²	Water	Clear
Seals graffiti and stains from spoiling a topcoat.	11 m²	Water	Clear
Seals dusty concrete floors. Hardwearing.	10 m²	White spirit	Basic colours
Concrete sealer. Must be overpainted.	10 m²	White spirit	Clear
Thick finish applying decorative patterns.	6 m²	Water	Brilliant white and pale colours

Paint

Type	Inside or out	Use	Application
Special purpose paints: (cont.)			
Universal sealer	Interior/Exterior	Plaster, concrete, chipboard, hardboard	Brush
Blackboard paint	Interior	Wood, metal	Brush
Insulation paint	Interior	Plaster	Brush
Lacquer	Interior	Wood, metal, plastic	Brush
Yacht enamel	Interior/Exterior	Wood	Brush
Child-safe paint	Interior/Exterior	Wood	Brush/Pad
Anti-rust primer	Exterior	Metal	Brush
Anti-condensation paint	Interior	Plaster	Brush/Roller
Hammered metal paint	Interior/Exterior	Metal	Brush
Radiator paint	Interior	Central heating radiators	Brush
New plaster paint	Interior	New plaster	Brush/Roller
Wood treatments:			
Knotting	Interior/Exterior	Wood	Brush
Creosote	Exterior	Sheds and fences	Brush/Spray
Woodworm killer	Interior/Exterior	House timbers	Brush/Spray
Wood hardener	Interior/Exterior	Wood	Brush
Wood preservative tablets	Interior/Exterior	Rot-susceptible timbers	—
Fungus treatments:			
Fungicide	Exterior	All exterior surfaces	Brush/Spray
Fungicidal spray	Interior/Exterior	Tiles, window frames, walls	Pump spray
Mould killer	Interior	As above	Brush/Sponge/Cloth
Dry rot killer	Interior/Exterior	Timber, brick	Brush/Spray
Chemical strippers:			
Paint stripper	Interior/Exterior	Wood, metal	Brush
Varnish stripper	Interior/Exterior	Wood	Brush
Paste stripper	Interior/Exterior	Wood, particularly mouldings.	Brush
Surface preparation:			
Sugar soap	Interior/Exterior	All painted surfaces	Sponge
Liquid sander	Interior/Exterior	Liquid sander	Sponge
Brush cleaners:			
Branded brush cleaner	—	Oil paints	—
White spirit (Turps substitute)	—	Oil paints	—
Cellulose thinners	—	Cellulose paints	—
Methylated spirits	—	Certain specialized paints	—
Fillers:			
Interior cellulose filler	Interior	Plaster, wood	Filling knife
Exterior cellulose filler	Exterior	Wood, brick, cement rendering	Filling knife
Mixed exterior filler	Exterior	Wood, brick, cement rendering	Filling knife
Fine surface interior filler	Interior	Painted and unpainted wood, plaster	Filling knife
Wood filler	Interior/Exterior	For woods to be varnished	Filling knife
Flexible exterior wood filler	Exterior	Wood only	Filling knife
Grain filler	Interior/Exterior	Open-grained hardwoods	Cloth
Wood finishes:			
Teak oil	Interior/Exterior	Unvarnished hardwoods, especially teak	Cloth pad
Tung oil	Interior/Exterior	Untreated hardwoods	Cloth pad
Beeswax	Interior	As above	Cloth pad
Silicone wax polish	Interior	Fine wooden furniture	Cloth pad
French polish	Interior	Hardwood furniture	Special pad

Paint

*Coverage depends on the surfaces and is for rough guidance only.

Properties	Coverage* (per litre)	Brush cleaner/Thinner	Colour range
Seals porous surfaces prior to painting.	12 m²	Water	Clear
Matt black and non-reflective. Ideal for old beams.	10 m²	White spirit	Black
Reduces heat loss through walls.	10 m²	Water	Brilliant white
Mirror gloss. Very hard. Ideal for bicycles and toys.	12 m²	White spirit	Bright colours
Contains aluminium flakes for waterproofing.	12 m²	White spirit	Basic colours
Non-toxic paint. Ideal for toys and cots.	12 m²	Water	Few colours
Contains anti-rust pigments for extra protection.	8 m²	See pack	White and grey
Inhibits condensation and mould growth.	10 m²	Water	Few colours
Attractive metal finish. Anti-corrosive.	5 m²	Cellulose thinners	Black, white and metallics
The heat helps this paint cure to a durable finish.	12 m²	See pack	Brilliant white
Allows new plaster to dry out through the surface.	12 m²	Water	Pale colours
Seals live knots to avoid spoiling paintwork.	—	Meths	—
Toxic to plants until solvents have evaporated.	3 m²	Water	Brown
Penetrating liquid for treating woodworm infestations.	4 m²	Water	Clear
Special resins bond and harden softened wood.	—	—	Clear
Tablets are inserted into drilled holes.	—	—	—
Kills mould, fungi, lichen and algae on walls.	22 m²	—	Clear
Useful in bathrooms and kitchens for killing mould.	—	—	Clear
Use prior to decoration on problem areas.	—	—	Clear
Kills the spores of dry rot fungus.	1 m²	—	Clear
Softens gloss paint. Will not soften emulsion.	4 m²	See can	—
Softens all types of varnish.	4 m²	See can	—
Apply as a putty. Peel off with old paint.	—	Water	—
Leaves painted surfaces clean and ready for repainting.	—	—	—
Wipe on. Cleans and keys painted surfaces.	—	—	—
Various brands available through DIY stores.	—	—	—
Cheap and readily available brush cleaner.	—	—	—
Available from auto accessory shops.	—	—	—
Readily available from hardware stores. Many uses.	—	—	—
Fine powder for mixing as required. Keeps well.	—	—	Dries white
As above but coarser.	—	—	Dries white
A thick paste for immediate use.	—	—	Dries white
Very fine. For an immaculate finish before painting.	—	—	Dries white
Available to match common hardwoods and pine.	—	—	Wood colours
Adapts to seasonal movement of exterior woodwork.	—	—	Grey
Stops varnish sinking into open grain.	—	—	Wood colours
Keeps exterior, untreated hardwood in good condition.	—	—	Clear
Natural satin finish which enhances the grain.	—	—	Clear
Natural wax finish for fine furniture.	—	—	Clear
High gloss finish for modern furniture.	—	—	Clear
Kits available. Certain skills needed.	—	—	Deep red and brown

Ceramic tiles

Estimating quantities

Ceramic tiles come in so many different sizes from all around the world now that the best plan of action is to visit the various DIY stores and Tile Merchants in your area until you find what you are looking for. Once you know the size of your preferred tile you can easily work out the number required by counting the rows and columns of your tiling area.

Tile types and shapes

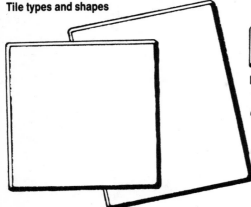

At the same time work out the area in square metres for buying your tile fix and grout cement. A six kilogram tub will fix and grout about four square metres.

Adhesives

There are two types of tile adhesive. Ordinary wall tile fix and grout for normal kitchen and bathroom areas, and shower and floor tile adhesive for heavily wetted areas.

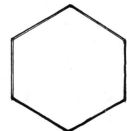

Border tiles

These will usually match rectangular tiles either for width or breadth.

Grouting

Grouting is usually done with the fix and grout adhesive, but tile grout is available separately and this is useful where a coloured grout is required.

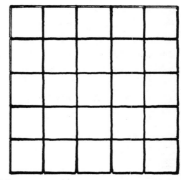

Mosaic

These come on an open mesh backing for easier installation. Individual tile size is usually 57 ×57 mm (2¼ ×2¼ in).

Plain square or rectangular

The commonest type of wall tile. Usual sizes are 150 ×150 mm (6 ×6 in), 150 ×200 mm (6 ×8 in) and 200 ×200 mm (8 ×8 in).

Tile edge trim

In plastic or metal of various colours, the bead covers the raw tile edge on a sill or corner. Available as 1.83 m (6 ft) lengths.

Bath edge trim

A soft flexible plastic moulding with a feather edge to seal against the bath. The upper part is set under the last course of tiles.

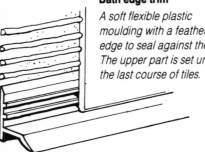

Hexagon

These make an interesting pattern when in place on a wall. Usually 100 mm (4 in) across. A mosaic version is also available.

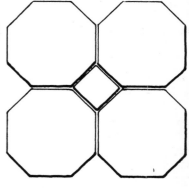

Interlocking tiles

The small centre tile (called tozzetto) is usually a contrasting colour and the whole set is usually sold in a pack sufficient to cover a square metre.

Provençale/Decorative shapes

Various interlocking shapes and sizes are often available from specialist importers.

Ceramic tiles

Tiles for special purposes

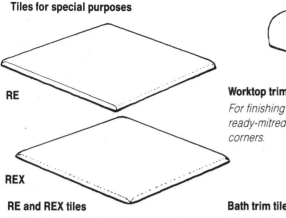

RE

REX

RE and REX tiles

RE tiles have one edge glazed while REX tiles have two edges glazed. Used on sills and external corners.

Worktop trim tile

For finishing a tiled worktop. Also available ready-mitred, for inside and outside corners.

Bath trim tile

For edging over the bath, this tile is tending to be superseded by flexible plastic trim to match modern lightweight baths.

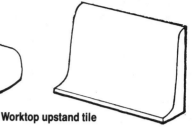

Worktop upstand tile

For finishing the back edge of a tile worktop. A more robust version is available for kitchen and bathroom floors to match quarry tiles.

Tools for tiling

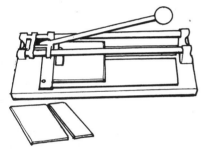

Tile cutting machine

This may seem expensive, but when set against the cost of broken tiles this tool is well worthwhile. With a built-in squared measuring gauge, a hardened cutting wheel and a tile cracker, very accurate cuts can be made even in heavy, thick floor tiles.

Oporto cutter

After scoring, by the hardened cutting wheel, the tile is placed in the jaws and snapped cleanly along the scored line.

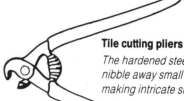

Tile cutting pliers

The hardened steel jaws can be used to nibble away small pieces of tile when making intricate shapes.

Spirit level

For setting accurate vertical and horizontal battens before starting tiling.

Tile scorer

Used with a try square, the tungsten carbide tip will score the glazed surface for a clean break.

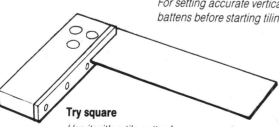

Try square

Use it with a tile cutter for square cuts.

Dowel rod

A piece of dowel rod filed to a smooth point can be used to finish grouting neatly.

Plastic spacers

Using these small spacers at the corner of each tile ensures accurate spacing over the whole tiled area.

Mesh tile trimmer

An open mesh abrasive for cleaning broken edges of tiles.

Floor coverings

Carpet laying is best left to the experts as they will do it quickly and be responsible for any problems that may arise. If you really want to do it yourself, start with a small bedroom where errors won't be so noticeable. A much easier alternative is carpet tiles. (See right.)

Carpet types

Carpets are roughly classified as follows:

Method of construction: tufted, woven and bonded.

The way the pile is treated: cut, looped and twisted.

The type of base material: hessian-backed and foam-backed.

The pile treatment is further classified as follows:

Hair and Woolcord. Tightly woven yarn giving a hardwearing if somewhat coarse feel.

Standard short pile. The pile is cut short giving a level, regular feel. Available in woven and tufted forms.

Loop pile. The woven yarn is left uncut to form loops.

Twist pile. The yarn is twisted before weaving to give a springy feel.

Sculptured carpet. Woven or tufted with a mix of cut and looped pile.

Velvet. Luxurious and very dense cut pile. It shades where the surface is disturbed.

Shag pile. A long, cut pile. Can be awkward to clean.

Berber carpet. Dense, looped wool pile with an ethnic air.

Note. Axminster and Wilton, two familiar names, are simply named after the looms on which they are woven.

How fitted carpets are secured

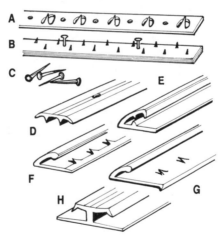

Carpet grippers are nailed around the floor, about 6 mm ($\frac{1}{4}$ in) away from the skirting board. The carpet is pulled tight over the gripper, whose prongs hold it securely, and pushed down into the gap between the skirting board and the gripper.

Choose the right underlay

A good underlay will make a significant difference to how your carpet wears. Reputable carpet stores will naturally fit the right type if they are fitting. The cost of underlay

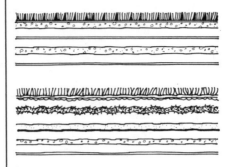

should be included in the estimate along with floor grippers and threshold bars. If fitting yourself use this guide.

Foam-backed carpet

Either Paper felt underlay
or Foam rubber underlay
and Paper felt underlay

Hessian-backed carpet

Either Soft felt underlay
or Hessian-backed rubber underlay (essential for stairs)
or Foam rubber underlay
and paper felt to stop it sticking to the floor (only for light wear)

Carpet-laying accessories

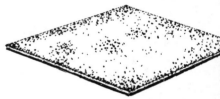

A. Gripper for foam-backed carpet.
B. Gripper for hessian-backed carpet.
C. Carpet tacks for odd corners.

Binder bars

Available in aluminium or brass finish, these are 813 mm (2 ft 8 in) long (to fit between doors) and can easily be cut with a hacksaw if too long.

D. Cover strip for carpets between doors.
E. Bar for foam-backed carpet.
F. Bar for hessian-backed carpets.
G. Bar for joining carpet to vinyl etc.
H. Cover strip for carpets between doors.
I. Knee kicker (right).
A specialized tool for stretching carpets when laying.

Carpet tiles

Sizes

500 × 500 mm (19 $\frac{11}{16}$ in sq) is the commonest size, but you may also find 305 × 305 mm (12 in sq) and 457 × 457 mm (18 in sq).

Carpet tiles have several advantages over broadloom carpeting—certainly as far as self-laying is concerned. They are extremely quick and easy to lay, require no underlay, are easy to fit even around door frame mouldings—you can cut one tile at a time. They can also be moved around to equalize wear and, being made of polypropylene, are stain-resistant.

Another advantage to the DIYer is that they can be taken up when decorating.

They are ideal for children's rooms and kitchens — where most spillages occur. They are not as soft to bare feet as conventional carpets but you can always put a rug down.

Should an accident occur just take up the tile and scrub it. If it's irreparably damaged swop it for another one under a piece of furniture.

Floor coverings

Sheet vinyl

Sheet vinyl is available off the roll in widths of 2 m (6 ft 6 in), 3 m (9 ft 9 in) and 4 m (13 ft 1 in). There are several grades and cushioned vinyl is ideal for bathrooms and bedrooms as it has a soft feel. Vinyl does require a flat surface for laying as any unevenness will show through. Timber floors should be overlaid with hardboard. Use 600 × 1200 mm (2 ft × 4 ft) sheets which must be conditioned first (see page 29). Uneven concrete floors can be levelled using a special floor levelling compound.

Laying sheet vinyl accurately is not an easy job as it cannot be manipulated as easily as carpeting. For a really accurate fitting use the following method. Tape down large sheets of brown paper on the floor all around the room about 13 mm (½ in) away from the skirting board. Cut to fit round other obstructions, such as toilet pans, and make sure all the sheets are taped securely to one another.

Take a small block of wood roughly 25 mm (1 in) across one dimension and, holding this against the skirting board with a pencil or felt-tip pen held on the other side, push it all around the room, marking the paper with a continuous line. Mark in obstructions carefully. Carefully lift the joined pieces of paper, take them to a larger room and then spread them over the sheet vinyl and tape down.

Taking the same piece of wood, you then go around the plan, drawing a line on the vinyl 25 mm outside of your plan.

Double check any obstructions marked in. You now have an exact copy of the floor area, with all its imperfections marked ready for cutting.

Use a sharp Stanley knife on a piece of hardboard and cut slightly oversize. Check the vinyl in position and make any adjustments for a perfect fit.

Draw around a five pence piece for 15 mm central heating pipes.

I. Knee kicker

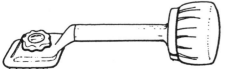

Vinyl tiles

Vinyl tiles are an easier way of laying a vinyl floor, but it's even more important to have a smooth surface. Hardboard on wood floors and self-levelling screeds on concrete floors will provide a good sub-floor. The vinyl tiles that are sold nowadays are often self-adhesive. Just peel off the backing paper and lay.

Size. Vinyl tiles are usually 300 × 300 mm (12 × 12 in).

Cork tiles

Cork is a natural material and has the advantage of feeling soft and warm to the touch. Two types of cork tile are available: natural finish and ready-sealed. The natural finish will require sealing after laying (see page 16). Sizes vary, so check the size available at your source for estimating quantities.

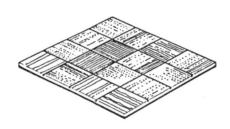

Wood flooring

Wood flooring, being more permanent than other types, requires a near perfect sub-floor. A timber floor in poor condition could be replaced with tongue-and-grooved flooring-grade chipboard (see page 29). Concrete floors may require a self-levelling screed.

The commonest type for DIY laying is the square parquet panel. They are self-adhesive and some are ready sealed with strong acrylic polymer coating, requiring no further work. They consist of strips of hardwood laid in a basket-weave fashion on a felt or fabric backing. The sizes and hardwood type vary according to source and they are usually sold in packs to cover a specific area.

Also available, although not so readily, is tongue-and-grooved wood strip flooring. This requires more work to lay but looks very attractive.

Sanded floors

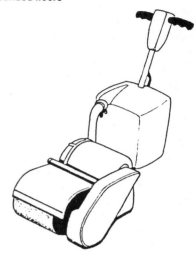

If you live in an older house and have attractive wooden floors it's worth considering sanding and varnishing them to reveal their lovely colours.

Gaps between the floorboards need to be filled with thin wooden strips or papier-mâché, and nail heads must be punched down. A heavy-duty floor sander can be hired which makes the job a lot easier.

A scattering of rugs completes the decor and once you have achieved a good finish you won't want to cover a floor like this. Varnishes and floor seals are listed on page 14.

Tip

Profile gauge

This will give you an instant and accurate copy of intricate shapes such as door mouldings which can then be marked on to cork, vinyl, wood or ceramic tiles, or sheet vinyl to give a perfect fit.

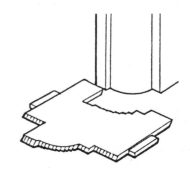

Window dressing

There is a variety of tracks and poles which can be used for hanging curtains, and to make the best use of your windows—such important features in a room—it is necessary to seek out the proper type for the effect you aim to achieve.

A. Plastic café rod.
For net and café curtains. Available either with support brackets or spring-loaded to fit between the window recess.
The flattened 'O' section resists sagging.

B. Brass café rod
For café curtains and nets. Telescoping tubes adjust to the window width. With end finials and brass support brackets.

C. Basic plastic track
Inexpensive track for use behind pelmets and valances.

D. Plastic track with hidden runners.
General purpose track particularly suitable for curtains with deep headings. Can be bent to fit bay windows.

E. Corded track
Avoids handling the curtains.

F. Valance rail
Designed to fit over the existing curtain track. With extended brackets.

G. Combined valance and curtain track
Two tracks in one pack for both curtain and valance.

H. Ruche track
Designed for Austrian, Roman and festoon blinds.

I. Hinged rod
Specifically for dormer windows where space may be insufficient at the side of the window to draw back the curtain. The curtain is swung aside on the pole and kept in place with a hold-back.

J. & K. Decorative wooden poles
Available in white and hardwood stains and in different diameters and lengths. Poles can be easily cut to your exact length. Poles are designed to be seen, with the curtain hanging below rather than in front as is the case with tracks.

K1. Flexible joint
For fitting poles around bay windows.

K2. Wooden ring
Turned wooden rings in colours and stains to match the poles.

L & M. Decorative brass poles
Similar to wooden poles, there are also versions which have a flat back incorporating a curtain track.

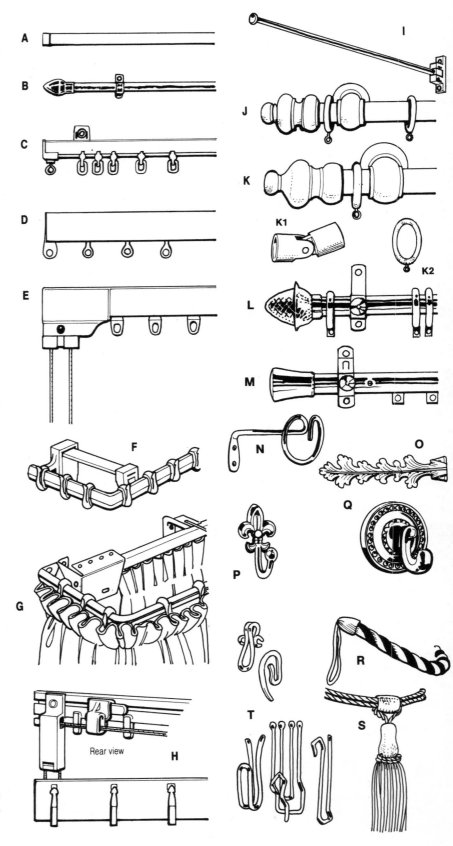

Rear view

Window dressing

Accessories

N. Swag hook

For holding decorative swags in position.

O. Brass plume hold-backs

Decorative hold-backs.

P. Fleur-de-lys brass tie-back hooks

Q. Heavy brass Georgian tie-back hooks

R. & S. Rope tie-backs

Silken-type tie-backs in various colours.

T. Assorted curtain hooks

Different curtain tapes require different hooks. Get the correct sort when you buy your curtains.

Curtain tapes

All curtains should be bought or made much wider than the curtain track so as to allow fullness when drawn. Skimping on width creates a harsh, stretched look. Different tapes have different requirements. The recommended widths are given in the following list. The curtain heading will pleat in a different way according to the type of tape fitted. Use the cheaper standard tapes where the heading will be hidden behind a valance or pelmet and the more decorative types for open display.

A. Standard pleats

Suitable for all curtain types and fabrics. Fabric width 1½ times the track.

B. Pencil pleats

Suits all types of curtains particularly modern styles. Fabric width 2½ times the track.

C. Triple pleats

Suitable for full-length curtains, particularly velvet. Fabric width twice the track length.

D. Cartridge pleats

Good for thicker, lined curtains. For better pleat definition stuff each pleat with rolled-up tissue paper. Suits modern plain fabrics, especially velvet. Fabric width 2½ times the track.

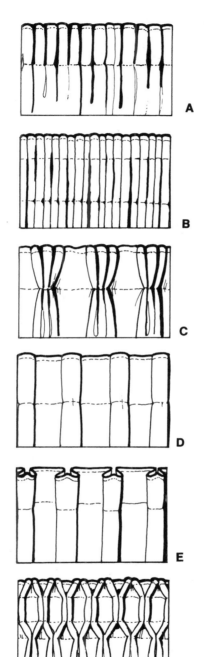

E. Box pleats

As above.

F. Smocked pleats

Suits traditional styles. Good for valances. Fabric width twice the track width.

Measuring a window

To measure a window for curtains the pole or track (**A**) should ideally be in place. Failing this, mark the position exactly and work from this. Tracks and poles should be fixed about 125 mm (5 in) above the top of the window recess, with space left either side of the recess to allow the curtains to be drawn back.

Note. It may be hard work drilling into the concrete lintel above the window, so consider fixing a wooden batten, secured by a few screws instead. The track supports can then be screwed to this. The batten can be painted to match the wall. It may be easier to fix to the ceiling joists if the ceiling is close to the top of the window.

For tracks measure from the top of the track and for poles measure from the eye on the ring.

For curtains and blinds inside the recess, measure at **B** for the width and **C** for the height.

For sill–length curtains outside the recess measure at **D** minus 12 mm (½ in).

For below sill–length measure at **E**. If a radiator is fitted stop short by about 20 mm (¾ in).

For floor length measure at **F** minus 25 mm (1 in) to clear the floor.

Plaster

Plastering on anything but a small scale is one of those jobs best left to a professional as badly done it can look awful. This is perhaps why textured finishes are so often applied by amateurs. Small cracks and holes are best treated with a cellulose filler (see page 16) and rubbed down, if necessary, when dry.

If you intend to do large plastering jobs consider using plasterboard, otherwise study a good book on the subject and observe the recommendations concerning types and thickness of various plasters. Buy from a source with a steady turnover as old plaster has an unnerving tendency to go off too rapidly, making it unworkable. Removing old plaster is a very messy job creating lots of dust. Wear heavy gloves, eye protection and a face mask.

Types of plaster

Different surfaces require different types of plaster according to their porosity. Use this table as a guide. When estimating quantities always err on the generous side.

Type	Use	Maximum thickness	Setting time	Coverage	Bag size (kg)
Browning plaster	Undercoat on semi-porous surfaces such as brick and lightweight block construction	11 mm ($\frac{7}{16}$ in) Apply two coats if the hole is deep	1½–2 hours	4½–5¼ m² (48–56 sq ft) per 35 kg bag	50, 40 35, 12.5, 7.5
Bonding plaster	Undercoat on dense surfaces such as concrete and clinker blocks.	8 mm ($\frac{5}{16}$ in) Apply two coats if the hole is deep	1½–2 hours	4–6 m² (43–64 sq ft) per 40 kg bag	50, 40, 20
Finishing plaster	Finishing coat on undercoat plasters	2 mm ($\frac{3}{32}$ in)	1½ hours	10–11 m² (107–118 sq ft) per 40 kg bag	50, 40, 12.5, 7.5, 2.5
Board plaster	Finishing coat on plasterboard	5 mm ($\frac{3}{16}$ in)	1½–2 hours	6–7 m² (64–75 sq ft) per 40 kg bag	50, 40, 20
One-coat plaster	Special DIY all-in-one plaster for use on concrete, breeze-block, brick, plasterboard and cement/sand finishes	75 mm (3 in)	½–1 hour	2–2.5 m² (22–28 sq ft) at 6 mm ($\frac{1}{4}$ in) per 10 kg bag	40, 20, 12.5, 10

Plasterboard

If you lack the necessary plastering skills but still want to cover large areas yourself, consider dry-lining—using plasterboard on battens. This is a good alternative for old ceilings, as by using the correct side out, all that is required to finish the job is a ceiling paper or a coat of emulsion. Bear in mind that large sheets of plasterboard can be heavy and will require possibly three people to manoeuvre and secure them in place. Use the proper plasterboard nails (see page 72).

Avoid baseboard if you don't want to try plastering, as this requires a skim coat of plaster to finish it. Wallboard has two faces: the grey side is for plastering over and the white side has a smooth finish for papering or painting. Go over the joins and nail heads with a cellulose filler for a perfect finish. Using a special sealer before papering will minimize damage to the plasterboard surface if you need to soak off the wallpaper in the future.

Plasterboard sizes

Plasterboard is generally available in the following sizes:

Baseboard. Square-edged grey board for finishing with plaster. 1200 mm ×900 mm × 9.5 mm (4 ft ×3 ft ×$\frac{3}{8}$ in).

Wallboard. Two different surfaces. One for plastering over and the other for direct decorating. In square edge and tapered edge. 1800 mm ×900 mm ×9.5 (6 ft ×3 ft × $\frac{3}{8}$ in). 2400 mm ×900 mm ×9.5 mm (8 ft × 3 ft ×$\frac{3}{8}$ in). 2400 mm ×1200 mm ×12.5 mm (8 ft ×4 ft ×$\frac{1}{2}$ in).

Tools

There are only a few specialized tools required for plastering and these are shown here.

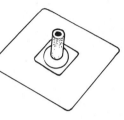

Wooden float

Use this to finish the undercoat, giving it a grainy texture that will provide a good surface for the topcoat to adhere to.

Plasterer's trowel

Good ones have a spring steel blade riveted to an aluminium alloy frame and a hardwood handle. Blade size is usually 255 mm × 120 mm (10 in × 4¾ in). An excellent tool for applying both undercoat and finishing plaster. Can also be used for exterior rendering.

Plasterer's hawk

This is used to carry the mixed plaster to the wall. Aluminium ones can be bought but you can make one up out of a piece of ply about 300 mm (12 in) square and a length of broom handle.

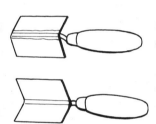

Internal and external corner trowels

Used for finishing the angles of walls which is always difficult.

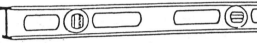

Builder's level

Get one at least 900 mm (36 in) long with two vials—one for horizontal checking and the other for checking plumb. They are useful for all sorts of DIY jobs.

Scratcher

Something else you can make yourself from six nails knocked into a timber offcut and with their heads cut off. This is used to scratch the surface of the partly dried undercoat to provide a good key for the finishing coat.

OTHER TOOLS

Spot board

A large piece of thick ply or chipboard about one metre square (3 ft × 3 ft). This is used to dump the plaster on after it has been mixed in the plastic bucket.

Two plastic buckets

One to hold clean water and the other to mix the plaster in.

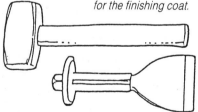

Club hammer and bolster chisel

These will be necessary if you are removing old plaster from the walls. Wear goggles and heavy gloves when using these tools.

Wide brush

An old distemper brush is ideal. Use this to flick water on to the wall prior to plastering.

Timber straightedge

1.5 m × 75 mm × 25 mm (5 ft × 3 in × 1 in). For levelling plaster between battens.

Timber battens

For setting out plaster levels on walls. 12 mm × 12 mm (½ in square).

Other items
Corner reinforcing bead

These are metal strips which are nailed to the wall corner before plastering. They provide a neat strong finish to the corner.

Joint tapes and scrim tapes

These are used over the joins in plasterboard before either skim-coating or filling tapered boards with joint filler.

Timber

Softwoods and hardwoods

The terms 'softwood' and 'hardwood' can be misleading. Softwoods, classified as coming from coniferous or evergreen trees such as pine, spruce, fir and larch, are generally found in the northern hemisphere and are the woods most likely to be used by the home woodworker.

Hardwoods come from deciduous trees, which take much longer to mature and are at risk from deforestation. There are both European types, such as oak, beech and ash, and tropical types, such as mahogany and rosewood.

Some softwoods can be hard like yew for example, and some hardwoods can be soft, such as balsa.

Softwoods are cheaper and more readily available in a greater range of sizes. They are used for construction and painted work, whereas hardwoods are used where their colour and grain variations can be exploited—such as with furniture.

Look in specialist woodworking magazines for hardwood suppliers.

Terminology

Deal
A piece of timber 50–100 mm (2 to 4 in) thick and less than 280 mm (11 in) wide.

Sawn
Sawn to the size quoted, with rough faces.

Planed
Planed smooth from the sawn size – although the size quoted is still the sawn size.

P2S
Planed two sides.

Dressed
Another term for planed.

PAR or DAR
Planed all round or dressed all round.

Joinery grade
Better quality softwood for most general woodwork.
May be further classified into Best joinery and Joinery.

Carcassing
Lesser quality wood for rough structural work where the wood will be hidden. Can also be used for garden construction.

Timber sizes

Although a timber yard will cut wood to your exact requirements, they charge more and so it is useful to know the standard sizes wood comes in when you plan your jobs. The chart opposite gives the commonly available sizes.

Sawing patterns of logs

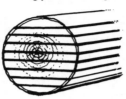  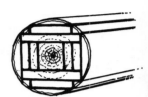

Through and through
The log is sawn into parallel planks. An economical method, but the outer planks can warp badly.

Quarter sawn
More wasteful but the planks come closest to the ideal, with the grain pattern resisting warping.

Tangentially sawn
Produces wide planks from relatively small logs.

The metric foot

Wood comes from the sawmill in metric lengths. For this reason timber merchants will quote in multiples of 300 mm or 11¾ in. If you ask for a 'six foot length', you may get 1800 mm or 5 ft 10½ in. Check when you order.

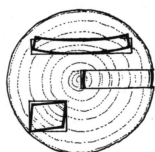

How sawing affects warping in planks

All new softwood will shrink. But by looking at the end grain you can anticipate in which direction and take it into account when planning your construction.

Big DIY stores often sell planed softwood shrinkwrapped. As these places are usually warm and dry, and the wood may have been in stock some time, any warping has usually reached its peak and you can select accordingly.

Faults in wood

Look for the following faults when buying wood and reject the wood if the faults cannot be cut out or will mar your work.

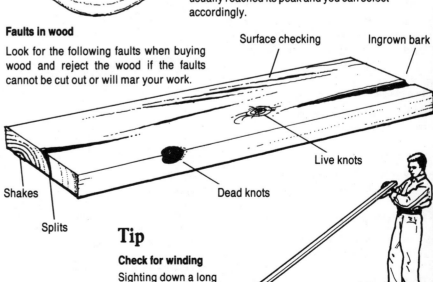

Surface checking — Ingrown bark — Live knots — Dead knots — Shakes — Splits

Tip
Check for winding
Sighting down a long piece of timber will reveal twisting.

Timber

Sawn and finished timber sizes

The drawing, right, shows an actual size timber cross-section of 115 mm ×38 mm (4½ in ×1½ in) in both its sawn and finished sizes. A loss on each face of approximately 3 mm (⅛ in) is due to the machining process plus shrinkage.

Even planed it will still be described as 115 mm ×38 mm.

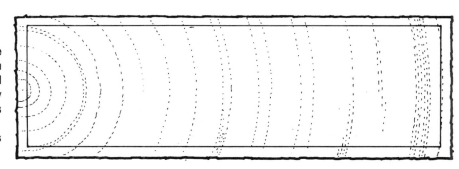

The table shows commonly available softwood sizes.

Some outlets will carry more, some less.

When working out your requirements allow

3 mm less per face for finished sizes.

A timber yard will machine a piece of wood to your exact requirements, but you will have to pay extra if it is machined from a

larger sawn size.

The greater the width of a plank in relation to its thickness, the greater the chance of the wood warping.

Thickness mm	Width mm										Thickness inches
	75	100	125	150	175	200	225	250	300		
16	*	*	*	*							⅝
19	*	*	*	*							¾
22	*	*	*	*							⅞
25	*	*	*	*	*	*	*	*	*		1
32	*	*	*	*	*	*		*	*		1¼
38	*	*	*	*	*	*		*	*		1½
44	*	*	*	*	*	*		*	*		1¾
50	*	*	*	*	*	*		*	*		2
63		*	*	*	*	*					2½
75		*	*	*	*	*	*	*	*		3
100		*		*		*		*	*		4
150				*		*			*		6
200						*					8
250								*			10
300									*		12
	3	4	5	6	7	8	9	10	12		
	Width inches										

Ramin PAR and dowel sizes

Ramin, although not a softwood, is a light coloured almost grainless wood. It is available in smaller sizes than softwood and is

often displayed in a 'mouldings bar' at DIY superstores.

mm	9	12	18	22	35	47	72	100
6			*	*	*	*		
9	*							
12		*						
18			*					
22				*		*	*	*

Round dowel: All 2.4 m long   6 mm, 9 mm, 12 mm, 18 mm, 25 mm

Hardwood, usually Philippean mahogany, is generally available off the shelf for specific house building purposes such as window sills and doorsteps.

Stock	50 ×25
"	50 ×50
"	75 ×50
"	75 ×75
"	100 ×50
"	100 ×100
Step sill	150 ×60
Window board	230 ×25

Manufactured boards

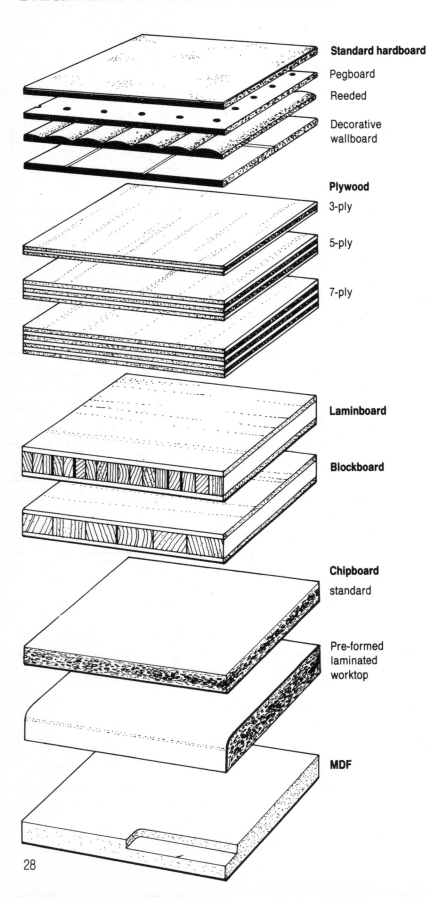

Standard hardboard

Pegboard

Reeded

Decorative
wallboard

Plywood

3-ply

5-ply

7-ply

Laminboard

Blockboard

Chipboard

standard

Pre-formed
laminated
worktop

MDF

Used extensively by the furniture industry, manufactured boards are a great boon to the home woodworker as well. It is important to select the correct type for the job you are planning and also to understand the properties that different boards have.

Although lacking the tensile strength (resistance to bending) of real timber, most boards offer perfectly flat, wide surfaces with a freedom from warping and shrinking.

There is an enormous number of different types of board manufactured for special purposes and some are only available to industry. Those described here are readily available at DIY superstores and large timber merchants. Most boards come in very large sheets and are impossible to transport by car, even on a roof rack, but fortunately most stores offer a cutting service which reduces them to more manageable proportions.

Hardboard

Hardboard is a dense, thin, brown board made from shredded and pulped timber. It is one of the cheapest boards available and the standard type has one smooth flat side, while the reverse carries the imprint of the wire mesh used in the manufacture.

It is useful for cabinet backs, drawer bottoms and makes a good subfloor under sheet vinyl.

Grades

Apart from the standard grade, the following types are available.

Double-sided. Flat on both surfaces.

Tempered. Treated with oil, this type can be used externally. (The standard type will buckle and soften if used in damp situations).

Pegboard. Supplied with holes drilled at regular intervals over the whole surface, this is particularly suitable for hanging tools etc. Special wire clips are available to fit the holes.

Perforated. With various geometric designs cut through the board these can make very attractive screens.

Reeded. Surface moulded during manufacture, this type provides a more interesting look than the standard board.

Decorative wallboards. Available in large sheets, designs such as tiles, tongue and groove cladding, bricks, etc. are imprinted on to the surface.

Manufactured boards

Conditioning hardboard

Hardboard can buckle when used in large sheets, especially for flooring, and should be conditioned before use. Spray the back with cold water and leave the boards in the room where they are to be used for 48 hours before fixing.

Plywood

More expensive than either hardboard or chipboard, plywood is made from actual wood veneers glued at right angles to one another with, usually, an odd number of plies. This gives a relatively thin, light board of high tensile strength in both directions.

The quality of plywood varies enormously and it can be difficult to cut a clean edge on the cheaper grades. The plies can be of equal or differing thickness and the numbers run from three, five and seven upwards.

Chipboard

This is one of the most familiar boards, coated with either real wood veneers or melamine, and makes excellent shelves. It is also found in the thicker contoured version with a decorative plastic laminate bonded on for kitchen worktops. It is made from chipped timber pressed with a resin binder into flat sheets. It blunts normal woodworking tools very quickly so any cutting should be done with TCT (Tungsten carbide tipped) blades. These boards are heavy and need special chipboard screws and methods for joining. (See page 30.) Often the centre core is made from coarser chips than the surface areas, so care is needed when drilling blind holes as the resistance to the drill can lessen, suddenly causing a break through.

Blockboard and laminboard

Less common than previously because of the emergence of the newer types of manu-factured boards, these use a more natural wood construction.

These boards consist of a core of rectangular strips of wood sandwiched between two veneers. In blockboard the core strips are usually from 8 mm to 25 mm ($\frac{5}{16}$ in to 1 in) wide, giving a better quality board.

MDF (Medium density fibreboard)

The newest and potentially most exciting of the manufactured boards. Light brown in colour, smooth on all surfaces, MDF is made from timber reduced to a fibrous state, impregnated with resin binders and compressed and rolled to its finished thickness.

What makes MDP so interesting is that it can be machined and cut as easily as a good quality timber without breaking up. It can also be painted or stained and varnished with similar effects to real wood. This is the only manufactured board that requires no edge treatment after cutting to cover vulnerable and raw areas.

Sizes of manufactured boards

Material	Thickness	Standard board
Hardboard (Including decorative wallboards)	3 mm ($\frac{1}{8}$ in) Thicker grades sometimes available	1220 × 2440 mm (4 ft × 8 ft) Smaller sizes equally divided from standard sheet.
Plywood	3 mm to 25 mm ($\frac{1}{8}$ in to 1 in)	1220 × 1220 mm (4 ft × 4 ft), 1220 × 2440 mm (4 ft × 8 ft), 1525 × 3050 mm (5 ft × 10 ft)
Blockboard and Laminboard	13 mm ($\frac{1}{2}$ in), 15 mm ($\frac{5}{8}$ in), 19 mm ($\frac{3}{4}$ in), 25 mm (1 in)	1525 × 3050 mm (5 ft × 10 ft), 1220 × 2440 mm (4 ft × 8 ft) Smaller sizes equally divided from standard sheet.
Standard chipboard	15 mm ($\frac{5}{8}$ in), 19 mm ($\frac{3}{4}$ in)	1220 × 2440 mm (4 ft × 8 ft)
Melamine and wood-veneered boards	15 mm ($\frac{5}{8}$ in)	In 2440 mm (8 ft) and 1830 mm (6 ft) lengths and the following widths. 150 mm (6 in), 230 mm (9 in), 305 mm (12 in), 380 mm (15 in), 460 mm (18 in), 530 mm (21 in) and 610 mm (24 in)
Decorative laminated worktops	30 mm ($1\frac{1}{4}$ in)	500 mm × 3050 mm ($19\frac{3}{4}$ in × 10 ft)
Flooring grade T & G (Tongue and Grooved)	19 mm ($\frac{3}{4}$ in)	610 mm × 2440 mm (2 ft × 8 ft)
T & G loft boards	19 mm ($\frac{3}{8}$ in)	405 mm × 1220 mm (16 in × 48 in)
MDF (Medium density fibreboard)	4 mm ($\frac{5}{32}$ in), 13 mm ($\frac{1}{2}$ in), 15 mm ($\frac{5}{8}$ in)	1220 mm × 2440 mm (4 ft × 8 ft) Smaller sizes equally divided from standard sheet.

Chipboard fittings

Because of the increased use and availability of chipboard throughout industry and the DIY market, a whole range of special screws and connectors has appeared over recent years.

Ordinary woodscrews should not be used as the threads are too fine and they will pull out or distort chipboard. Special chipboard screws, which look similar to self-tapping screws, are available and some are described here. The great majority are designed for the standard 15 mm ($\frac{5}{8}$ in) thick chipboard either for fixing to, or for fixing together.

Note. Some of the connectors described require large, shallow blind holes drilled into the surface. The ideal tool for this is the hinge sinker described on page 77.

Chipboard screws

Available as countersunk or pan-head and in various lengths, these require pilot holes to avoid splitting the ends of chipboard panels. Try several drill sizes on a scrap piece of chipboard until you find one that drives easily and holds firmly.

Hi-lo screw

A strong screw made from carbon steel with a double thread. Cover caps available. Available in the following lengths; 33 mm ($1\frac{1}{4}$in) and 45 mm ($1\frac{3}{4}$in).

Confirmat screw

A thick screw with a heavily buttressed cylindrical thread. Available in one size only. It requires a 7 mm ($\frac{9}{32}$in) through hole and a 5.5 mm ($\frac{7}{32}$in) pocket hole in the end of the panel to be joined.

It will pull a board up tightly and make an extremely strong fixing.

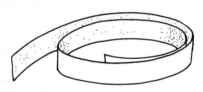

Edging strip

After cutting melamine surfaced chipboard an ugly raw edge is exposed. This self-adhesive strip, available in various widths, will match the surface finish of the board. It is applied using a domestic iron.

Shelf supports

Plastic shelf suppport

A 10 mm ($\frac{3}{8}$ in) diameter blind hole is drilled into the inner side of a cupboard, the hollow plug is pushed in, then the shelf support is inserted up to the shoulder, flat side up. Four of these will support an average kitchen cupboard shelf.

Brass shelf support

A brass socket is pushed into a hole in the side frame and the ring plug inserted. The shelf rests on the exposed part of the ring plug.

Panel connectors

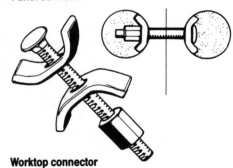

Worktop connector

Designed for fitting under worktops, this connector will butt up end panels very tightly. It requires a pair of blind holes and a slot between the two.

Cabinet connector

A simple connector which bolts through the sides of two cabinets to lock them together.

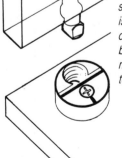

Cam fitting

An 8 mm ($\frac{5}{16}$in) hole is drilled into the end of the vertical panel to accept the cranked nylon dowel which is then locked with a steel pin. A 25 mm (1 in) diameter blind hole is drilled in the horizontal panel to take the circular boss. When the two panels are brought together, a half turn on the screw moves the cam and locks the panels together.

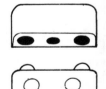

Block joint

After careful marking each part is screwed to its relevant panel, then both are pulled together with a machine screw.

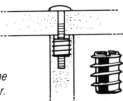

Screw socket

Used in either the ends or surfaces of panels, the screw socket is driven into an 8 mm ($\frac{5}{16}$in) hole with a screwdriver, using the slots provided. A machine screw is then screwed into the internal thread to provide a secure fixing.

Timber connectors

Most of the connectors and fittings shown on this page can be used either on solid timber or manufactured boards.

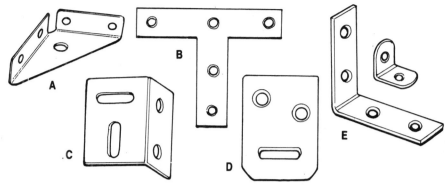

Metal plates

A. Corner bracket

Very useful for hanging wall cabinets, as the top and sides can be secured by chipboard screws, whilst a longer screw can pass through the back and into the wall.

B. T bracket

Used for strengthening frames etc.

C. Angle bracket

Simple, straightforward brackets which are useful for construction in hidden areas.

D. Shrinkage plate

These plates are designed for joining timber planks where the slot allows for movement of the timber. They are also useful for joining manufactured boards.

E. Corner braces

Various sizes available of these useful angle brackets, although they don't have a great resistance to distortion.

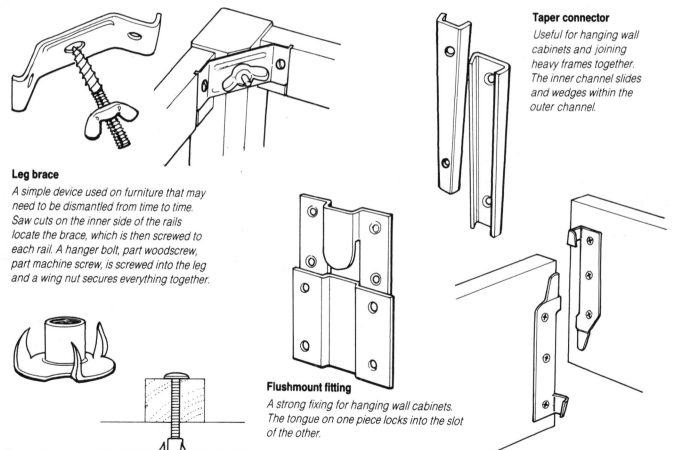

Leg brace

A simple device used on furniture that may need to be dismantled from time to time. Saw cuts on the inner side of the rails locate the brace, which is then screwed to each rail. A hanger bolt, part woodscrew, part machine screw, is screwed into the leg and a wing nut secures everything together.

Pronged tee nut

Used with a bolt of suitable length, the pronged tee nut bites into the wood to provide a simple connector. Preferably used on softwood.

Flushmount fitting

A strong fixing for hanging wall cabinets. The tongue on one piece locks into the slot of the other.

Taper connector

Useful for hanging wall cabinets and joining heavy frames together. The inner channel slides and wedges within the outer channel.

Bed frame fitting

Designed for beds which need to be dismantled, but is useful for other heavy frame construction.

31

Tools

The range of tools available for working in wood is vast and some have very specialized uses. The tools shown on these two pages are the basic ones necessary for getting started in woodwork.

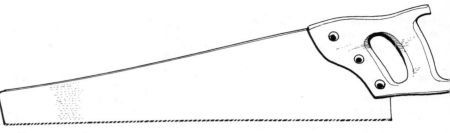

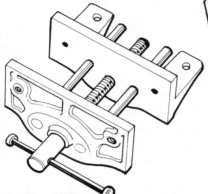

Woodworkers vice

Woodworking vices are available in a range of sizes. Buy the biggest you can afford. The metal faces are drilled and should be fitted with 10 mm (⅜in) ply, cut slightly larger than the vice. Clamp-on versions are also available if you don't have a permanent bench.

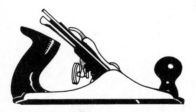

Smoothing plane

There are many types of plane, both metal and wood, but the basic metal smoothing plane is the most useful. Quality planes last a lifetime and will produce a fine finish on all types of wood.

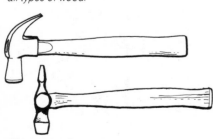

Hammers

Two basic designs of hammer are used in woodwork; the claw hammer and the cross-pein hammer, both available in various weights. See pages 72–3.

Handsaws

The large handsaw is available in three different types; the crosscut saw is designed for cutting across the grain, the ripsaw is for sawing along the grain and the panel saw for manufactured boards. However the powered circular saw is now widely used for all three purposes and these saws are now only purchased by craftsman.

Try square

A good quality try square is essential for marking accurate right angles and checking frames after gluing.

Marking gauge

This is used for marking a line parallel to the edge on a piece of timber, as, for example, before planing down. The sliding stock is locked by a thumbscrew and once set, measurements can be repeated on other workpieces.

Workmate bench

Beloved of jobbing builders and DIYers everywhere, the Workmate will handle a variety of jobs. The full length vice top will cope with irregularly shaped workpieces, while large panels and doors can be clamped in the ends and rest on the floor. It lacks the rigidity of a fixed bench, but folds flat for storage after use.

Tenon saw

This saw is indispensable for preparing even simple joints. The back is braced with a heavy brass or steel support to keep the blade true.

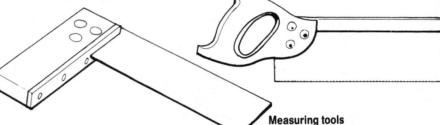

Measuring tools

Either a steel expanding tape measure or the traditional boxwood folding rule will be found useful. Whichever you choose, try to obtain one with dual imperial/metric markings.

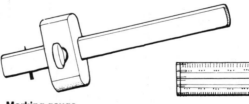

Tools

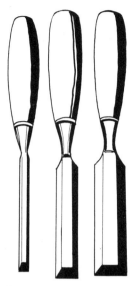

Chisels

It's probably best to buy chisels as and when needed, but a basic set of three in the following size range will cover most general needs. 6 mm ($\frac{1}{4}$in), 19 mm ($\frac{3}{4}$in) and 38 mm ($1\frac{1}{2}$in).

Mallet

Usually made from beech, this is used to drive a chisel for chopping out mortises etc. Never hit a chisel with a hammer, the handle could be irreparably damaged.

Bradawl

Used for starting holes before drilling, it can also be used instead of a drill for small screws in softwood.

Bench hook

These are available in shops but they can easily be made from scrap ply. They are very useful to steady short lengths of timber when sawing ends etc.

Mitre box

There are many designs of mitre boxes, some in hardwood, some with metal guides, others in plastic or metal. They all aim to help the woodworker cut the perfect mitre, one of the most difficult joints to make accurately. The slots guide the saw at the correct angle.

G cramp

Sooner or later you will need something to hold wood while you work on it, which is too large for the vice, so you can't have too many of these. Very useful also for holding joints while the glue sets. Sizes range from 50 mm (2 in) openings, up to 300 mm (12 in). 100 mm (4 in) is a useful size.

Combination oilstone

With one side fine and one side coarse, this is an indispensable accessory to your toolchest. Lubricate with light oil and use it often to keep your tools sharp.

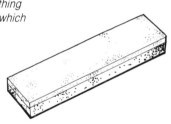

Woodworking adhesive

For simple interior joints, latex woodworking adhesive in a handy applicator pack will be found useful. For exterior work use a resin powder. See pages 80–81 for more information on adhesives.

Twist drills

A set of High Speed Steel twist drills will serve for both wood and metalworking. Sets from 1 to 10 mm ($\frac{9}{16}$ to $\frac{3}{8}$ in) in 1 mm increments are handy. Further information on drills can be found on page 37.

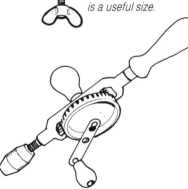

Hand drill

Although the ubiquitous electric drill is used almost universally, a hand drill is much more controllable for the smaller drill sizes. See pages 37 for full coverage of drill types.

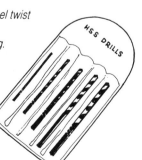

HSS DRILLS

Countersink

Necessary for sinking countersunk screws flush with the surface.

Tools 2

When you become more involved in the pleasures of working with wood you will start to assemble a more comprehensive range of tools. Those shown here — although not a complete range — will give you some idea of what is available from specialist tool shops.

Block plane

With its blade set at a much lower angle than the smoothing plane, this tool is specially designed to cut end grain.

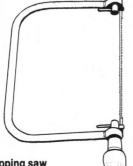

Dovetail saw

Smaller than the tenon saw, this finely-toothed saw assists in the cutting of accurate joints, particularly in hardwood.

Spokeshave

As its name implies, this was originally created for wheelwrights. It is very useful for cleaning up curves. There are various types available but the flat-bottomed version is most useful.

Coping saw

A useful saw for fine work, as the blade can be turned to face any direction.

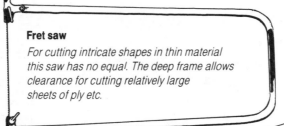

Fret saw

For cutting intricate shapes in thin material this saw has no equal. The deep frame allows clearance for cutting relatively large sheets of ply etc.

Rebate plane

Accurately machined on the base and two sides, this little plane will clean out sawn rebates beautifully. The nose portion can be dismantled, allowing one to get right into corners.

Marking knife

When working on fine cabinet making, a scored line can be more accurate than a pencil line. Using one of these with a try square will help greatly.

Sliding bevel

Useful for marking angles which may need to be repeated elsewhere, this tool works well used in conjunction with a try square.

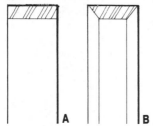

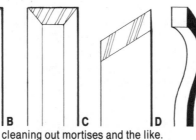

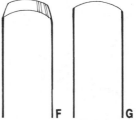

Types of chisels

There are many types of chisels, some for special applications such as woodcarving and turning. Those shown here are the basic shapes.

A. Firmer chisel
Firmer chisels are strongly made specifically for use with a mallet.

B. Bevel edge chisel
The bevels ground along the sides allow this chisel access into tight corners for cleaning out mortises and the like.

C. Paring chisel
An extra-long bevel edge chisel for getting into deep mortise slots.

D. Skew chisel
Useful on difficult grain or for cleaning out corners.

E. Lock mortise chisel
The curved blade allows one to clean out the bottoms of deep narrow mortises.

F. Out-cannel gouge

G. In-cannel gouge
A gouge is described as out-cannel when the bevel is ground on the outside of the curve. If ground on the inside, it is an in-cannel gouge.

H. Drawer-lock chisel
Designed to be hit with a hammer, this little double-ended chisel is used for chopping out drawer-lock mortises when access is difficult.

Tools 2

Carpenter's brace

The oldest type of drill still in common use, it is used with auger bits (see page 36) to cut large holes cleanly. A ratchet behind the chuck allows for a part sweep, when space is limited, in either direction.

Mortise gauge

A mortise gauge has two pins which are adjusted to the width of the mortise (slot) and which can then be marked in one pass and repeated on other workpieces.

Cabinet scrapers

These simple tools will remove wood in fine shavings without tearing the grain even on cross-grained woods, and provide a very fine finish. A smooth steel burnisher is used to turn over the edge, so forming a very fine hook.

Dovetail marker

Made of brass, these are used for marking dovetail saw cuts. The wider side is for softwood and the other for hardwood.

Edging cramps

Useful for holding glued strips in position on the edge of a board.

Webbing cramp

A simple, inexpensive frame cramp consisting of a length of webbing secured by a metal lever-operated ratchet.

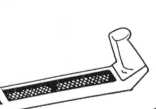

Surform files

An ingenious blade design characterizes the Surform range. The disposable flexible blade has perforations to allow rapid waste removal while the hardened ground edges will smooth and shape a range of materials from wood to mild steel. Many shapes available.

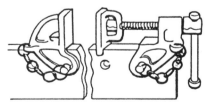

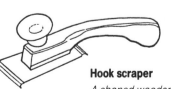

Hook scraper

A shaped wooden handle and replaceable hook blades make this tool a useful alternative to the cabinet scrapers mentioned above.

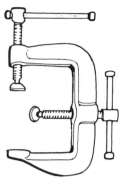

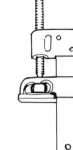

Sash cramps

A pair — or even four — of these useful cramps can make the gluing up of large items of furniture far easier. The rear stop can be moved along the bar to suit the size of frame being glued. To avoid marking the work use wood packing between the cramp heads.

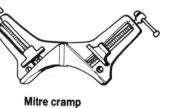

Mitre cramp

This cramp will adjust to the width of most mouldings, which is useful in gluing up picture frames for example.

Cramp heads

Similar in every way to sash cramps except that you make your own bars from hardwood battens.

Quick action cramp

A movable jaw slides along the serrated beam to produce positive locking action.

Auger bits

There's a large and sometimes confusing range of drill bits available. Most are designed for a specific purpose and this page describes the types in common use. Although carbon steel twist drills are perfectly suited to drilling wood, it's best to go for the slightly more expensive HSS (High speed steel) drills as these can then also be used for drilling metal.

When drilling metal, lubricate with light machine oil to cool the tip. Cast-iron requires no lubrication. The larger sizes of twist drills have a reduced shank to fit the chuck of DIY electric drills, which are usually 10 mm ($\frac{3}{8}$ in) or 13 mm ($\frac{1}{2}$ in).

Use a bradawl to mark softwood for drilling and a centre punch for hardwood and metal.

Hand-drill chucks will not usually accept drill shanks larger than 9 mm ($\frac{3}{8}$ in).

Drill bits with square tapered shanks are specifically for use in a brace.

All drill bits can be re-ground—even TCT tipped masonry drills (see page 41).

Bits used in a brace

    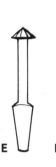  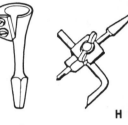

A   B   C   D   E   F   G   H

A. Centre bit. An inexpensive bit for drilling holes from 6 to 50 mm ($\frac{1}{4}$ to 2 in). Can only really be used for shallow holes as it tends to wander.

B. Solid centre auger bit. A strong bit which will produce deep straight holes.

C. Jennings pattern auger bit. This has a double helical twist pattern for easy chip ejection but it is not as strong as B.

D. Expansive bit. A considerable range of hole sizes can be drilled with the one bit by adjusting the sliding spur/cutter to the exact size required. Available in two sizes 12–38 mm ($\frac{1}{2}$–$1\frac{1}{2}$ in) and 22–75 mm ($\frac{7}{8}$–3 in).

E. Countersink. For sinking countersunk screws flush with the surface of the wood.

F. Screwdriver bit. If you have a carpenter's brace get one of these. They are invaluable

for removing stubborn, rusted-in screws.

G. Dowel sharpener. Used to sharpen the ends of dowels for easier insertion into drilled holes in cabinet making. See bottom right.

H. Tank cutter. Used to cut large holes in sheet metal and plastic cisterns. Also useful for making washers.

Scotch-eyed auger

This is a hand tool for use in situations remote from power supplies. A rod is placed through the eye and the bit is turned by hand. Used for drilling deep holes in fence posts and tree stumps. Sizes range from 6–50 mm ($\frac{1}{4}$–2 in) diameter.

Snail type countersink

This tool produces the neatest countersunk holes in wood when used in a hand drill.

Centre punch

For accurately locating the drill point when drilling in metal and hardwood, use one of these. A light tap with a hammer will produce a small indentation.

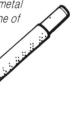

Gimlet

A very simple tool for drilling holes by hand in wood. Three sizes are available: 3 mm ($\frac{1}{8}$ in), 5 mm ($\frac{3}{16}$ in) and 6 mm ($\frac{1}{4}$ in).

Archimedean drill

Mainly used for model making because of its ability to drill very small holes. Moving the slide up and down produces rapid turning at the bit. The bits, called points, are stored in the handle and range from 1 mm ($\frac{3}{64}$ in) to 4.4 mm ($\frac{3}{16}$ in).

Electric drill bits

Electric drill bits

   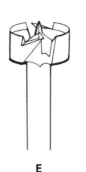 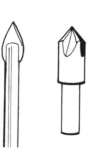 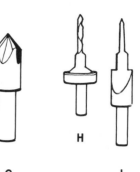 

A   B   C   D   E   F   G   H   I   J   K

A. HSS (high speed steel) twist drill. This is the most common type of drill bit and is used for all kinds of metals and wood. Metric sizes start as small as 1 mm and range through 1 mm increments to 10 mm: imperial sizes range from $\frac{1}{16}$ in to $\frac{1}{4}$ in in $\frac{1}{64}$ in increments.

B. Dowel bit. This twist drill has a point and two spurs and will give much better location in all woods and manufactured boards. Particularly good in end grain as it will not wander.

C. Masonry drill. This drill has tungsten carbide cutters brazed into the tip and it is used on a slow speed in a hammer drill to penetrate brick, masonry and concrete. Sizes start from 4 mm ($\frac{1}{16}$ in) up to 10 mm ($\frac{3}{8}$ in). Even larger sizes are available, but these usually require very powerful slow speed percussion drills to drive them.

D. Spade bit. Used for the rapid boring of larger holes in wood. Not a very clean cut. Sizes are from 6–38 mm ($\frac{1}{4}$ to $1\frac{1}{2}$ in).

E. Forstner bit. Expensive but produces exceptionally clean, flat-bottomed holes in wood. It will drill overlapping holes and partial holes at the edge of wood without wandering, as it is guided by the outside cutter and not by the point. Ideal for screen-work, scrollwork and scallops.

F. Glass drill. For drilling sheet glass, bottles, mirrors, tiles and ceramics. Use in a hand drill or an electric drill at slow speed and light pressure. Cool the tip with water or turps. Sizes available: 4–8 mm ($\frac{1}{8}$–$\frac{5}{16}$ in).

G. Countersink. Different types for wood or metal. For recessing the head of counter-sunk screws.

H. Drill and countersink bit. Available in sizes to match the common gauges of wood screws, these will drill the pilot hole, clearance hole and countersink in one operation.

I. Drill and counterbore bit. Similar to H, these will drill a counterbore hole for sinking the screw below the surface for covering with a wooden plug (see J).

J. Plug cutter. This cuts a neat plug of wood which will fit into a counterbored hole into which the wood screw has been driven. The plug is glued in and then planed flush, providing an almost invisible fixing.

K. Masonry drill extensions. Specially long masonry drills with screwed shanks are available and these can be further extended by fitting extension sleeves of 150 mm (6 in) or 305 mm (12 in). Considering house walls can range from 230 mm (9 in) to 305 mm (12 in) and above in thickness, these tools can be useful, but the amount you are likely to use one makes hiring a better proposition.

Dowelling jig

The favoured way of joining large boards is by using dowels and glue. The problem of locating the dowel holes accurately is overcome by using one of these jigs. There are various designs on the market and they are supplied with instructions for use.

Fluted hardwood dowel pins

These are available in three sizes: 6, 8 and 10 mm. The flutes give good keying for glue.

Metal depth stop

Clamped to the twist drill at the required depth, this will control drilling depth. In 6, 8 and 10 mm drill sizes.

Dowel locating pins

After drilling holes in one half of the joint, push the barrel of the pin into the holes, offer up the work accurately and tap the joints together. The precise position of the mating hole will be marked ready for drilling.

Sharpening techniques

All cutting tools need regular sharpening to operate efficiently. This applies to things like kitchen knives and scissors as well as planes, chisels and drills. There are many aids to efficient sharpening, ranging from electric knife sharpeners to powered bench grinders. However, a few good quality oilstones—or water stones—along with some small files will do everything you need. When using a powered grindstone take care to avoid overheating the cutting edge as this will draw the temper (hard-ness) of the steel. Constant dipping in water will help obviate this risk.

As a general rule the cutting edge is pushed along the stone rather than trailed and on bench grinders the wheel should be moving towards the blade (see A). This rule is reversed when stropping a blade on a leather or using grit-impregnated rubber grinding wheels. In these cases the blade is trailed (see D).

A flat combination oilstone with one side coarse and the other side fine, kept in a wooden box, is ideal for general purpose sharpening. Use the coarse side for re-grinding bevels when a blade is chipped—or if the honing bevel is getting too great—and the fine side for honing. Honing is the term used for putting the final cutting edge on a blade.

Powered grindstones are used dry, but oil-stones and slip stones should be lubricated with a few drops of light household oil before use. Water stones are soaked in clean water before use.

Sharpening chisels and plane blades

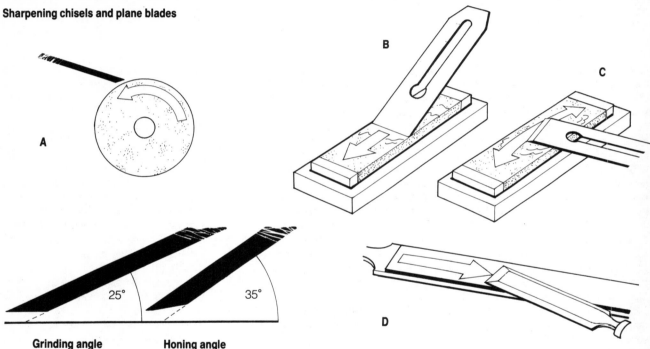

Grinding angle   **Honing angle**

The main bevel on both plane blades and wood chisels should be ground at approximately 25°. Some woodworkers will hone the fine cutting edge at this angle, but generally a secondary bevel of about 35° will give a more satisfactory cutting edge and is easier for repeated honing as less metal is being removed. Eventually the bevel will need to be re-ground at 25°. These angles are accurately shown above. For honing lay the blade iron or chisel, bevel side down, and raise it until the bevel feels flat on the stone. Raise it slightly more and move it forward over the oiled stone, slide it back and repeat (B). A plane iron will use the full width of the stone, but a chisel should be moved in a figure of eight pattern to equalize wear over the whole surface of the stone. Turn the blade over and lay it flat on the stone to remove any burrs (C). Finally give the blade a few strokes on a leather strop, this time working away from the cutting edge (D).

Sharpening gouges

A small, lightly oiled slipstone will be required for sharpening gouges. An out-cannel gouge—one that has the bevel ground on the outside—can be sharpened on a flat oilstone by running it, bevel side down, from side to side rolling it as you go.

Lightly remove burrs from the inside by a few strokes with a slipstone. An in-cannel gouge—one with a bevel on the inside—is sharpened by working a slipstone at about 30° on the inside. Finish the outside with a few strokes on a flat smooth stone.

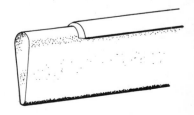

Sharpening techniques

Sharpening saws

Lots of saws are now available with hard-point teeth and these cannot be sharpened by hand. If you are buying for the first time go for one of these. They will stay sharp even when used on manufactured boards and when they do eventually wear can be easily replaced. Saw sharpening is a slow tedious business and angles must be maintained as well as the 'set'. The set of a saw is the way alternate teeth are bent outwards to give clearance in the saw cut (the kerf) and stop the saw binding. There are special pliers available for this purpose. The cutting angles are renewed using a small triangular saw file and different saws require different angles. The small dovetail saws can be particularly difficult to sharpen andd these need to be done professionally. Circular saw blades can be re-sharpened provided they don't have TCT teeth, but even these can be professionally sharpened. Ask in a good tool shop for the name of a local saw doctor.

Sharpening auger bits

Use a very small smooth file to sharpen auger bits. Sharpen spurs from the inside only or the circular shape will be impaired. Similarly, to maintain flatness the cutting edge should be sharpened underneath, on the bevel.

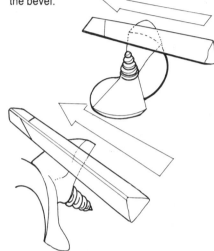

Twist drills

It's almost impossible to sharpen twist drills by hand because of their small size and critical angles. Also, the point can easily be ground off-centre. However, there are some excellent jigs on the market which will control the angles precisely (see next page). The smaller sizes of twist drill are impossible to sharpen and should be replaced when worn.

Dowel bit

Dowel bits can be sharpened using needle files on the spurs—observing the general principles mentioned under auger bits.

Spade bits

Using a small stone or fine file, renew the original bevels but don't touch the outside.

Kitchen knives

We have all admired the butcher, who with a few flashing strokes on his steel puts a razor edge on his well-worn knives. This, however, takes many years of practice to perfect. A simpler and safer way is to hold the steel, point side down on a chopping board, and, with the knife held at a slight angle, slide it from the base of the blade to the point in a smooth action as if you were trying to slice the steel itself. Then repeat on the other side of the steel. Do this every time you use your kitchen knives and they will serve you well. Eventually the knife will need to be re-ground and a grinding wheel is the best thing to use.

Sharpening scissors

If you look at the blades of a pair of scissors you will see a pronounced bevel at the cutting edge. This bevel must be maintained if cutting performance is not to be impaired. A small slipstone is the ideal tool to renew this bevel. If the edge is nicked or damaged a few strokes on the flat of the blade should help, but keep this at a minimum because if too much metal is removed here the scissor action will become loose. Note: if scissors are to be used for cutting cloth, resharpen using a file instead of a stone as this leaves a minute serrated edge which will grip soft fabrics better.

Garden shears

Grass-cutting and hedge-cutting shears can be sharpened like scissors. The same principles apply. Either a large file or a flat oilstone can be used. Clamp the blade in a vice to make the job easier and try to maintain the original bevel.

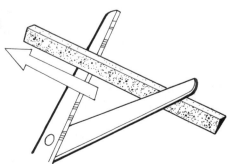

Tools

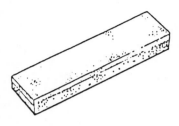

Combination oilstone

The basic sharpening tool. Lubricate with light oil and use it to keep all sorts of edge tools sharp. Use the coarse side for regrinding bevels and the fine side for honing. Finish by using a leather strop. These stones are usually 200 ×50 ×25 mm (8 ×2 ×1 in).

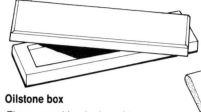

Oilstone box

These can either be bought or you can make your own. When not in use keep your oilstone in it to avoid attracting dirt and to protect it from damage.

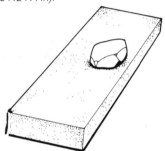

Japanese water stones

In recent years these stones have started appearing in this country. They cut quicker than oilstones but also wear more quickly. They range from very coarse to very fine.

Honing guide

It can be difficult to hold a true angle when honing blades on an oilstone. This little device rolls along with the chisel or plane iron clamped securely at the correct angle for perfect results.

Slipstones

These little stones are indispensable for all sorts of sharpening jobs. The rounded edge ones are necessary for sharpening gouges and the other shapes are useful for auger bits, scissors and knives. Lubricate with oil before use.

Saw files

Fine triangular files for sharpening saw teeth and auger bits etc. Available in a range of sizes.

Leather strop

These can be bought but they can easily be made by fixing an old leather belt to a piece of wood. A few finishing strokes on this after using the oilstone puts an extra keen edge on all tools.

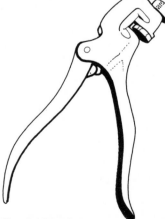

Saw setting pliers

These automatically set (bend) the teeth on crosscut, rip and tenon saws (except hardpoint saws) to the correct degree by adjustment of the numbered wheel.

Saw sharpener

The major problem associated with sharpening handsaws is maintaining the correct angle on the tiny teeth. This sharpening jig once set to a specific angle will file the teeth consistently and to a uniform depth along the whole length of the blade. Cannot be used on hardpoint saws.

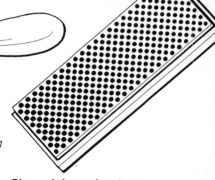

Diamond sharpening stones

These use diamond particles bonded into a plastic base. Three grades are available: coarse, medium and fine.

Tools

Arbor mounted grinding wheels

These can be used in an electric drill mounted in a horizontal stand for general grinding of knives and cold chisels. All sorts of sizes available.

Bench grindstone

There are various designs of bench grindstone available. The usual type has a fine wheel and a coarse wheel which both run at 3000 rpm and are typically powered by a $\frac{1}{4}$ hp motor. They have tool rests—one of which has an angled groove for positioning twist drills—and spark guards to protect the eyes. Useful for grinding cold chisels, screwdrivers etc. Care should be taken not to allow overheating when grinding edge tools, as this will affect the temper of the blade. Dip the blade in water repeatedly during grinding to cool it. Other models have a high-speed grinding wheel at one end and a slow-speed water-cooled stone at the other. Still others have flexible belts mounted on one end for sharpening and sanding.

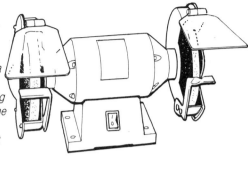

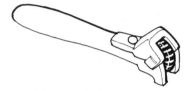

Star wheel dressing tool

When grinding wheels become glazed they will not cut properly. Holding this against the moving wheel resurfaces it.

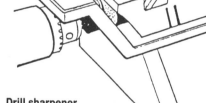

Drill sharpener

This helpful device screws onto the bench top and is driven by an electric drill. Although fiddly to set up, once in position it will grind all twist drills and masonry drills (using the alternate wheel). For this reason it's best to grind all your drills at one time rather than individually. Replaceable stones are easily obtainable.

Bench sander

This is mainly intended for sanding the end grain on wood, but its tilting table and right-angle stop make a good grinding machine with the correct disc. It clamps to the work table and is driven by an electric drill. Replacement discs are available.

Miniature grinding points

These little grindstones can be used in an electric drill or flexible drive for grinding intricate shapes.

Japanese whetstone grinder

Very expensive but you will never have a blunt tool in your hands again. With its large diameter, 200 mm (8 in) horizontal grinding area, a choice of stones—180 grit (very coarse), 400 grit, 1000 grit (for general grinding) and 6000 grit (for superfine finishing)—and its low running speed, this machine satisifies almost every sharpening need. Virtually all tools can be sharpened and stones are quickly interchangeable. Stones should be soaked for five minutes in clean water before use.

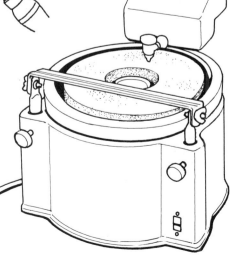

Nuts and bolts

Removable fastenings for metal

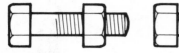

Nut and bolt

The bolt is only part-threaded. Found everywhere in various sizes for joining metal components together.

Set screw

A set screw is threaded for its whole length. It is screwed into a threaded hole to fix metal parts together.

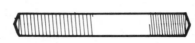

Stud

Threaded at both ends, usually one coarse and the other fine. One end is screwed into the work while the other end has a nut to secure a particular item.

Measuring bolts

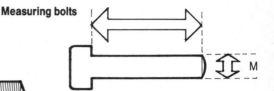

Bolts and screws are measured by the body length excluding the head—except in the case of countersunk heads where the entire length is measured.

The designation 'M' gives the outside thread diameter in mm. Washers also have their hole measured in this way. Thread cuts are either coarse or fine.

Head types

| Hexagon | Countersunk | Roundhead | Cheesehead | Instrument screw | Pan head | Grub screw | Allen screw |

Nut types

| Hexagon | Wing nut | | locknut | Cap nut | Elastic stop nut | Castellated nut | Spring steel nut |

Hexagon. Standard basic nut for use with spanners.

Wing nut. For removable fittings. Tighten by hand only.

Locknut. Used under standard nut to give extra security.

Cap nut. Used to hide the end of a bolt and give a decorative finish.

Elastic stop nut. A fibre insert locks against the thread to counteract vibration.

Castellated nut. Used with a split pin which passes through a hole in the bolt and has its ends splayed out.

Spring steel nut. Used with self-tapping screws to hold light sheet metal fixings.

Washer types

    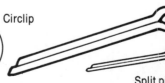

| Plain | Spring lock | Toothed | Round lock | Spring clip | Circlip | Split pin |

Plain. Available in a vast range of sizes. Used to spread the pressure over a larger area.

Spring lock washer. Made from spring steel. An anti-vibration device.

Toothed washers. These bite into soft mat-erial for extra grip.

Round lock washer. Matches a groove cut in the bolt shaft. Often used to fix adjust-ment on cone bearings.

Spring clip washer. Sprung into a groove cut around a shaft to secure light items.

Circlip. Spring steel. Sprung into a groove cut around a shaft or bore. Used to hold pulleys or bearings in position.

Split pin. Used with castellated nut (see above).

Spanners

ISO sizes

Most new bolts and screws manufactured nowadays are made to ISO standard metric sizes (International Standards Organization). However there are a lot of different imperial sizes from our industrial past. A brief description is given in case you come across them.

BSW. British Standard Whitworth
BSF. British Standard Fine
UNC. Unified Coarse Thread
UNF. Unified Fine Thread
BA. British Association
BSP. British Standard Pipe
BSB. British Standard Brass

Self-tapping screws

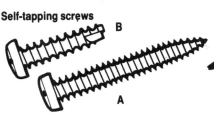

Self-tapping screws

Self-tapping screws are used everywhere, particularly in cars. They come in two distinct types: thread forming 'A' and thread cutting 'B'.

Thread forming is pointed and is used in soft materials only. Thread cutting is identified by a blunt end and has a flute cut part way into the thread. This can be used on all materials.

Drilled holes for self-tapping screws should be roughly 80% of the thread diameter.

Spanners

Spanners come in many shapes, sizes and sets, both metric and imperial. It's important to buy good branded tools. Cheap spanners will soon distort and cause endless frustration. If you can only buy a few, a good quality adjustable spanner will cover a range of sizes and be indispensable around the house. Don't use Stillsons on nuts (they are meant for pipes) or you will almost certainly round them off.

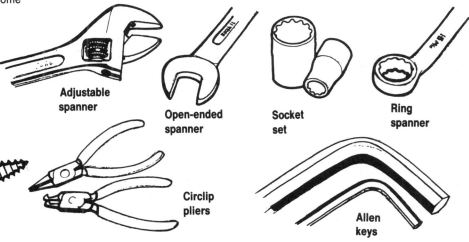

Adjustable spanner

Open-ended spanner

Socket set

Ring spanner

Circlip pliers

Allen keys

Spanners

Adjustable spanner. Adjustable spanners are available in a range of sizes and are a useful standby tool.
Open-ended spanner. The commonest type of spanner. Useful where access is limited.
Socket spanner. Usually bought as sets to cover a whole range of sizes. Used with a ratchet handle.
Ring spanner. An excellent cranked spanner which grips all round.
Circlip pliers. Special pliers for removing and replacing circlips.
Allen key. An 'L' shaped hexagon bar. Available singly or as sets in a large range of sizes.

Cleaning metal

For cleaning paint off metal, chemical paint strippers can be used, with coarse wire wool to get into the intricate areas (see page 16).

For cleaning unpainted metal you can use wire wool, emery cloth or wet-and-dry silicon carbide paper. The coarser grades of all of these abrasives will mark soft metal. To get a fine finish start with a coarse grade and use progressively finer grades until all the scratches are removed. Wire wool is particularly useful for getting into intricate shapes.

Wire wool grades

3–4.   Coarse. For cleaning down wood floors and rough metal surfaces.
1–2.   Medium. For general cleaning of wood and metal.
0.   Fine. For finishing wood and metal.
0000.   Very fine. For very fine finishing and polishing of metal.

Emery cloth grades

Available in coarse, medium and fine. Grade markings vary between manufacturers.
Standard sheet size: 230 ×280 mm (9 ×11 in).

Silicon carbide wet-and-dry paper

Available in coarse, medium and fine.
Standard sheet size: 230 ×280 mm (9 ×11 in).
Despite its name this should always be used wet.

Problem screws

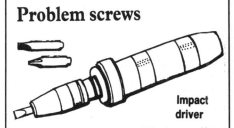

Impact driver

This tool comes with several bit sizes and is struck with a hammer to convert impact energy into torque and so loosen the most stubborn screw.

Screw extractor

For removing bolts or screws with damaged or sheared heads. A suitable hole is drilled in the centre of the screw and the tapered extractor, which has a left-handed (reverse) thread, is screwed in using a spanner. The force that is applied will eventually remove the offending screw.

Tools

METALS COMMONLY FOUND IN THE HOME

Mild steel

The most commonly used metal for manufactured articles. Easy to file, bend, saw and drill, it can also be soldered. Used for brackets, hinges, screws, nuts and bolts and in thin sheet for casing washing machines, refrigerators, freezers, etc. Corrodes rapidly if left unprotected.

Aluminium alloy

Light and easy to work. Used for kitchen utensils, handles and knobs, window frames and greenhouses. Does not easily corrode.

Cast iron

Strong and heavy, but brittle. Not easy to work. On older houses found as gutter downpipes and brackets, manhole covers and door and gate fittings. Also used for saucepans and stove parts. Corrodes very slowly.

Copper

Soft and easily worked and soldered. Used for plumbing pipes and fittings, saucepans and decorative items. Its excellent conductivity makes it useful for electrical parts and cables. Polishes well.

Brass

Heavy, strong and brittle. Resists corrosion and polishes well. Manufactured items like plumbing and heating fittings are often made in brass.

Lead

A very heavy, soft metal. Easy to work but lacking strength. Used for water pipes (in older buildings), roof flashings and solder. Does not corrode.

Wrought iron

Quite a lot of so-called wrought iron is actually mild steel, but you may inherit a pair of gates or some railings with an old house. Needs protection by painting.

Stainless steel

Strong and bright, but not easy to work. Resists corrosion well. Found as saucepans, kitchen utensils and cutlery.

Cast steel

Used for cutting tools and drills. Very hard, can only be ground by the amateur.

Tungsten carbide

Extremely hard. Used for the cutting tips of masonry drills and on saw blades and cutters for man-made boards.

With the amount of metal found in the home, the householder will need a basic understanding of how to work and use metal.

Ball-pein hammer

For general metalworking use. Head weights range from 113 g ($\frac{1}{4}$ lb) to 1.3 kg (2$\frac{3}{4}$ lb). 900 g (2 lb) is a good choice.

Engineer's pliers

For general gripping and bending of metal. 180 mm (7 in) is a useful size.

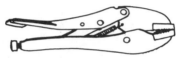

Mole wrench

A very useful tool around the house because, as well as being used as pliers, these can also clamp materials together and lock.

CUTTING SHEET METAL

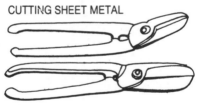

Tinsnips

Models available for straight cutting of sheet metal, or curved for cutting left- and right-hand curves.

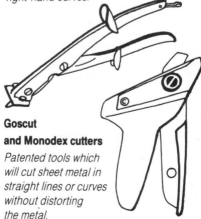

Goscut and Monodex cutters

Patented tools which will cut sheet metal in straight lines or curves without distorting the metal.

Engineer's vice

A strong heavy vice for metalworking. Don't use your woodworking vice for holding metal. Various designs available. Jaw widths range from 63 mm (2$\frac{1}{2}$ in) to 150 mm (6 in). Fibre jaws are available for gripping soft materials.

Try square and scriber

For accurate squaring of metal workpieces. The hardened tip of the scriber easily marks metal and plastics for accurate cutting.

Files

Three basic shapes—flat, half-round and round. Various sizes are available but 255 mm (10 in) or 305 mm (12 in) are the most useful.

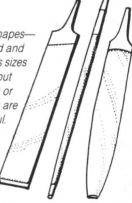

File cuts

Files are cut in three basic grades

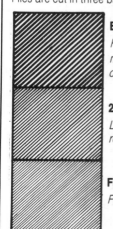

Bastard cut

For fast removal of material. Leaves a coarse finish.

2nd cut

Light removal with a reasonable finish.

Fine cut

For fine finishing work.

Tools

Hacksaws and blades

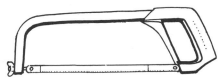

Standard frame

This will take 255 mm (10 in) or 305 mm (12 in) blades. Most are adjustable to take both. After taking up slack, turn adjuster two whole turns for correct blade tension.

Junior hacksaw

An inexpensive tool for occasional use. It takes 152 mm (6 in) blades.

Lubrication

Use lubricating oil to cool and ease cutting of hard materials (except cast-iron which needs no lubrication) and paraffin for soft materials.

HACKSAW BLADES

Selecting the right blade

Hacksaw blades are 255 mm (10 in) or 305 mm (12 in) long. For proper cutting make sure that at least three teeth are in contact with the material to be cut. Fit blades with the teeth facing forward. Blades are usually printed with information regarding type, number of teeth and recommended use.

BLADE SELECTION GUIDE

No. of teeth per 25 mm	Thickness	
	Hard material	Soft material
32	Under 3 mm	Under 3 mm
24	3–13 mm	3–6 mm
18	Over 13 mm	6–13 mm
14	—	Over 13 mm

BLADE TYPES

Bi-metal blades

Outstanding cutting with long life. A flexible blade allied to a High Speed Steel cutting edge gives good all-round performance.

Flexible blade

Flexible low alloy steel blade for soft materials only (aluminium or copper).

All hard

For the skilled user. Exceptional cutting but liable to break.

Blind riveting

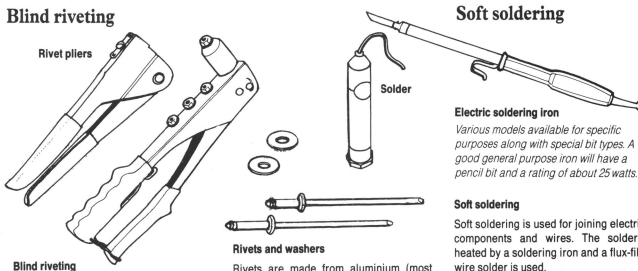

Rivet pliers

Solder

Blind riveting

Blind riveting is a quick and convenient way of joining sheet metal, particularly aluminium. Softer materials such as leather, thin plywood and plastics can also be riveted, but they will require washers to strengthen the join. The advantage of blind riveting is that access is only necessary from one side.

Rivets and washers

Rivets are made from aluminium (most commonly), copper and stainless steel. Common rivet diameters are 3 mm, 4 mm and 5 mm and all are available in long, medium and short, except 5 mm which is available in short and medium only. Rivets are usually boxed in quantities of 25, 50 and 100. Backing washers are available to suit all the common rivet diameters.

Soft soldering

Electric soldering iron

Various models available for specific purposes along with special bit types. A good general purpose iron will have a pencil bit and a rating of about 25 watts.

Soft soldering

Soft soldering is used for joining electrical components and wires. The solder is heated by a soldering iron and a flux-filled wire solder is used.

Soft soldering is also used for joining copper plumbing pipes (see p 61).

Soft solders are a mixture of lead and tin in various proportions and are available as small 2 m (6 ft) reels of 1.2 mm diameter, containing cores of flux for electrical work. 0.7 mm diameter flux-cored solder is also available for working on printed circuits.

Power tools

When electric drills first arrived on the scene, enterprising manufacturers produced all sorts of bolt-on equipment to widen their appeal. Most of these were underpowered and something of a compromise. They have now been superseded by high quality, self-powered tools often developed from industrial use. While power tools certainly take the hard work out of tedious jobs, like ripsawing long lengths of timber, they work so rapidly that scrupulous care is needed in setting up and using. A moment of inattention can ruin a carefully prepared piece of timber; therefore hand tools, although slower, are often preferable.

Using power tools safely

Always use a Residual Current Device plugged into the mains as this cuts off the power supply in a fraction of a second should a fault occur. See page 50. All power tools should be used with care. Most operate at high speed so manufacturers' safety instructions should be followed implicitly. Work should be held in a vice or clamped securely to a workbench. Eye protection should always be worn and in the case of grinders and power sanders a simple face mask with replaceable filters is a good idea.

Don't force circular saws as these can suddenly jam. Make several passes through thick timber going deeper each time rather than trying to cut at maximum depth in one go.

Electric drills

The electric drill is almost an essential in the modern home. Very few fixing jobs can be managed without one and drilling into brick walls is virtually impossible by any other means. Get one with a change-over hammer action and you will be able to tackle masonry drilling as well as wood and metal.

There's an enormous choice of electric drills available ranging in price from the single speed to the sophisticated, multi-featured top models.

An explanation of electric drill features.

1. Chuck. The capacity of the chuck refers to the maximum diameter of the drill shank that the tool will accept. Most domestic drills are either 10 mm ($\frac{3}{8}$ in) or 13 mm ($\frac{1}{2}$ in).

2. Chuck key. All drills come supplied with a chuck key. This turns the chuck and so controls the opening of the jaws and locks the drill bit in place.

3. Adjustable handle. Twisting the handle unlocks it, allowing movement to a convenient position for the user. It can be completely removed for mounting the drill in a stand or for using other attachments. A 43 mm diameter collar will allow the use of equipment from other manufacturers to be fitted.

4. Depth stop. This will control the depth of the drilled hole. Adjustment is made by unscrewing the handle slightly, thus allowing it to slide in or out.

5. Trigger switch. This starts the drill running when squeezed. In a variable speed drill there is a small turn button incorporated in the switch to control the speed.

6. Trigger lock button. After the trigger is squeezed this button can be pressed in to lock the drill for continuous running, as when the drill is used in a stand for example.

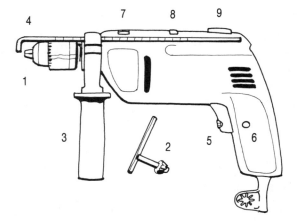

7. Hammer action selector. Sliding this switch across selects the hammer action. This is used at a slow speed for drilling into masonry.

8. Reverse action switch. With a slow speed selected the drill can be used to drive and remove screws. This switch reverses the direction of the chuck for withdrawing screws and can also be used to withdraw drills that have become jammed.

9. Torque control. This knurled knob controls the action of the drill to increased resistance. The drill will stop when it reaches the pre-selected torque. It also gives a slowly accelerating start for jobs such as starting screws etc., and protects the motor from overload.

Note

For extensive information on drill bits, see page 37.

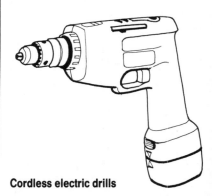

Cordless electric drills

Cordless drills are useful in that they can be used anywhere without the need for a trailing lead. They are not as powerful as mains-powered drills and cannot be used in vertical or horizontal stands but they do have the all-important hammer action.

Maximum capacities in current models are: wood—16 mm ($\frac{5}{8}$ in) and steel and masonry —10 mm ($\frac{3}{8}$ in). It's an advantage to buy two battery packs so that you don't run out of power halfway through a job.

Power tools

Drill accessories

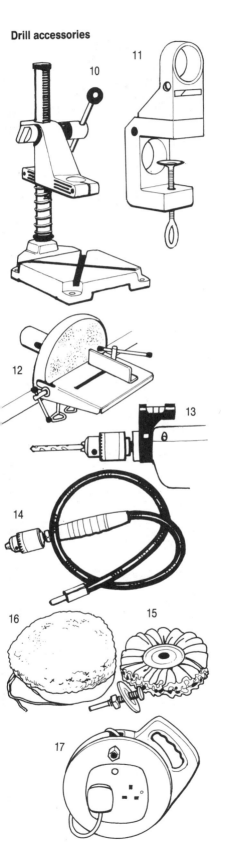

10. Vertical drill stand. A drill stand gives much more accuracy and control when drilling wood and metal. It can also be used for mounting a router.

11. Drill clamp. Various versions available. This one clamps the drill in several positions onto and alongside the bench.

12. Bench sander. This clamps to the edge of the bench and the drill is laid on its side and connected via the chuck. Velcro-backed sanding discs fit the rigid backing disc and the stop and the table can be adjusted to various angles. It is particularly good at providing an immaculate finish on end grain after sawing.

13. Horizontal drill guide. One of these can be useful as an aid to properly aligned holes, but you won't be able to use the front drill handle when this is attached.

14. Flexible drive shaft. One end fits into the drill chuck and the other end has a chuck to hold small grindstones and rotary rasps etc., for getting at confined areas.

15 & 16. Buffing pad and lambswool bonnet. The arbor-mounted felt pad can be used for buffing a surface and the lambswool bonnet, mounted over a rubber backing pad, will produce the final polish.

12. Extension lead. You literally can't go far without one of these. Most will have a safety cut-out to prevent overloads and some have two or more socket outlets.

Note

Different manufacturers all offer a similar range of power tools for the DIY market and although they look superficially similar to one another for tools like circular saws, jigsaws and planers the blades may not be interchangeable.

Take this into consideration before you spend a lot of money on a new power tool. Will there be sufficient back-up locally for you to obtain future supplies of replaceable items as well as service arrangements? From time to time there are blades on offer from independent suppliers. Check the packaging to ensure that they are appropriate for your make and model number.

Finishing tools

Electric planer. This rapidly removes wood via a revolving drum containing a pair of replaceable cutters.

Electric sanders

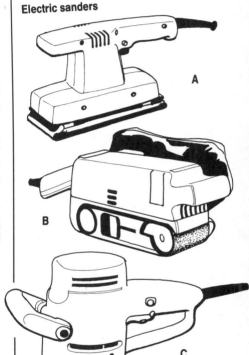

A. Orbital sander. Well established sander in which the flat base moves in tiny circles as the tool is pushed along the work. Some types can be changed over to a reciprocating action.

B. Belt sander. Larger, more powerful machines, in which a continuous belt moves over rollers to give rapid wood removal along the grain.

C. Multi-sander. A fairly new type, this has velcro-backed flexible discs. Although the action is rotary, it follows an eccentric pattern and this has been found to give an almost scratch-free finish. It can sand convex and concave surfaces equally well.

Power tools 2

Power saws

Circular saw. This is probably the second power tool, after the drill, that most home owners purchase. This will handle ripsawing and crosscut sawing with ease. It comes with an adjustable fence which runs along the board edge to give a consistent width of cut. Two versions, based on different blade sizes, are available; A 140 mm ($5\frac{1}{2}$ in) diameter blade gives a maximum cutting depth in timber of 40 mm ($1\frac{9}{16}$ in) and a 185 mm ($7\frac{1}{4}$ in) blade, a maximum depth of 62 mm ($2\frac{7}{16}$ in). The blade can be angled for cutting mitres and some versions have an outlet for connection to a vacuum cleaner for sawdust collection.

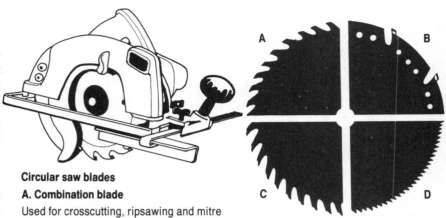

Circular saw blades

A. Combination blade

Used for crosscutting, ripsawing and mitre cutting in all woods. Can be re-sharpened.

B. Balanced TCT blade

For all woods but particularly good for manufactured boards which quickly blunt steel blades. Requires professional re-sharpening.

C. Multi-tooth TCT blade

General purpose cutting in all woods, plasterboard and plastics.

D. Fine-tooth blade

For thin plywood and plastics.

Jigsaw. Modern jigsaws are smooth, powerful and quiet. They are more user-friendly and safer than circular saws although they take longer to cut. Some models have an orbital action which means that the saw blade swings back on the down stroke to clear the wood, so lessening the amount of friction. Jigsaws with variable speed control will handle metal sawing with particular ease. Most jigsaws will cut up to 54 mm ($2\frac{1}{8}$ in) in wood and 3 mm ($\frac{1}{8}$ in) in steel.

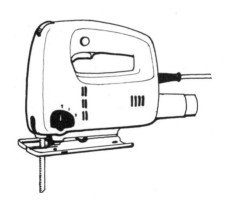

Jigsaw blades

Power saw blades cut on the upstroke—including circular saws—so when cutting laminates turn the work over and mark and cut from the underside unless using blade I.

E. Fast fine wood cutting

F. Coarse wood cutting

G. Very fast wood cutting

H. For cutting up to an obstruction

I. Reverse tooth for laminates

J. Scroll cutting

K. Coarse metal cutting

L. Fine metal cutting

M. Tungsten carbide for ceramic tiles

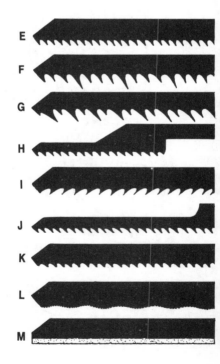

All-purpose saw

There are several designs of this saw on offer from different manufacturers which can be considered a general purpose and garden saw. Different blades are available for cutting wood, metal, plastics, plasterboard and even lightweight concrete blocks. The blades can be rotated to cut upwards and sideways. Will also cut curves.

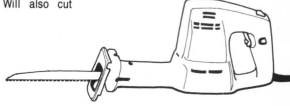

Power tools 2

Plunging router

Even if you do only a modest amount of joinery you will find one of these sophisticated tools invaluable. They have a collet chuck which takes a very wide range of shaped cutters to produce all sorts of mouldings quickly, and because they revolve at very high speeds, cleanly.

As well as hand-held operations they will also fit a 43mm diameter drill stand—turning the router into a mini-milling machine.

Router cutters

There's a huge range of cutters available and the basic shapes are shown here. Some are available with TCT cutting edges for work on manufactured boards but these will need professional re-sharpening, whereas the high-speed steel cutters can be sharpened on a slipstone (see pages 38–41).

Cutters fall roughly into two types: grooving cutters which will cut different-shaped grooves into flat boards and, edge-forming cutters which shape the edge in various ways.

Grooving cutters
A. Straight cutter
Buy the double-fluted type as this will give a better finish.
B. Veining cutter
C. Core-box cutter
D. V-grooving cutter
E. Dovetail cutter
Can be used with a special jig to make dovetail joints.
Edge-forming cutters
Edge cutters can have a fixed tip, which may burn the edge of the wood requiring further finishing, or a ball-bearing tip which makes the cutter more expensive.
F. Rebate cutter
G. Laminate trimmer cutter
This cleans the edges of plastic laminates flush with the edge of the board.
H. Chamfer cutter
I. Rounding-over cutter
According to how it is set this will either produce a simple rounded edge or a stepped rounded edge.
J. Beading cutter
K. Coving cutter
L. Roman ogee cutter

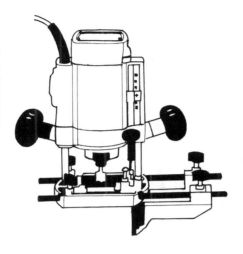

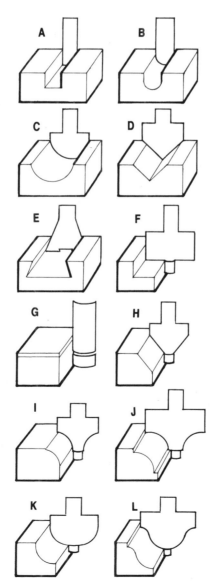

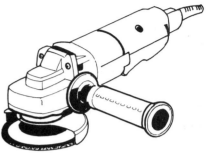

Angle grinder. Carborundum discs will cut through difficult materials like stone, concrete and tiles. It is also useful for grinding metal and some types can be used for sanding and wire brushing.

Workcentres

To further increase the repertoire of portable power tools there are on the market various workcentres into which you fit one or more power tools. These will turn, for example, an electric saw into a table saw or a router into a spindle moulder. These workcentres, although ingenious, are no match for the machine tools they aim to imitate but they do have the advantage of costing a great deal less. If you want to consider one of these then try to visit a tool shop where they will demonstrate the workcentre rather than buying it off the shelf.

Machine tools

If you are considering buying a purpose-made machine tool only you can decide if the amount of work will justify the cost. You will also need to do some homework by reading up on the various types available to see which is most suitable for your particular needs. Look in the local library for books on setting up a workshop. Local tool shops often advertise demonstration days when they operate the various machine tools in stock and can give expert advice. You will also get a chance to try these machines yourself under their guidance. Any fixed equipment will require a firm base in a secure workshop with room to move and extra good lighting. When buying, stick to well-known names and be suspicious of special offers which may mean a manufacturer is going out of business.

Distribution

Distribution

The electricity supply enters the house either by overhead or underground cables, passes through the Electricity Board's main fuse and then to the Board's meter. From the meter it goes to the fused consumer unit. This can consist of either rewireable fuses, cartridge fuses, or miniature circuit breakers (MCBs).

From the consumer unit the supply is distributed throughout the house in the following ways. One circuit passes under the ground floor, connects to all the ground-floor sockets, and back to the consumer unit. This is known as the ring circuit or ring main. A second circuit serves the upper floor in a similar way. In a small house these two circuits may be combined. Lighting circuits travel to all the lights and switches via the ceiling and roof spaces. Finally, individual radial circuits run to single, high-consumption units, such as cookers, immersion heaters and instantaneous electric showers.

Reading your meter

If you have a modern digital meter, then simply note the current reading and deduct the previous reading from your bill to give the number of units used. If you have a dual meter, the row of figures marked 'LOW' are for your use of cheaper, night-rate electricity and the row marked 'NORMAL' are for units consumed at the day rate.

Dial meters are harder to read, but once understood are straightforward. Note that adjacent dials run in opposite directions.

Starting with the dial on the left, write down each number that the pointer is actually on or has just passed, not the figure nearest to it. Important. If one of the figures is a '9', reduce the previous figure by one. Ignore the dial marked 1/10. The reading below would be 44928.

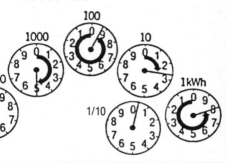

Plugs

Standard moulded plastic plug

The standard way to connect movable appliances to sockets. Manufacturers are increasingly supplying appliances with plugs already fitted.

Moulded rubber plug

Use where the plug is likely to be dropped on hard floors such as, for example, with power tools and garden equipment.

Easy plug

A large ring moulded into the body of this plug makes for easier handling by those with weak or arthritic hands.

Plug adaptor

For connecting more than one plug to a single socket. Beware of overloading sockets.

Electrical terms

AC/DC
Alternating current/Direct current. Mains electricity is AC and batteries are DC.

Amps/Amperes
Measurement of electrical current.

Double-pole switch
On/off switch that isolates both the live and neutral side. Most ordinary light switches are single-pole.

Gang
Term for the number of individual switches on a single accessory.

IEE Wiring Regulations
The Institute of Electrical Engineers' guidelines for safe installation practice.

kWh
Kilowatt/hour. One unit of electricity. Your electricity bill is calculated using this as a basis.

Ohms
The measurement of electrical resistance.

Voltage
The measurement of electrical pressure. UK supply is 240v.

Watts
The measurement of electrical consumption.

Residual current device (RCD)

Also known as an Earth Leakage Circuit Breaker (ELCB) and a Residual Current Circuit Breaker (RCCB).

This indispensable device cuts off current in a fraction of a second if it detects a sudden leakage to earth due to a fault. Always use one when working outside or using power tools.

Tools

ELECTRICAL SAFETY
Warning. Mains electricity can kill!

Do not attempt any electrical work unless you are sure you know what you are doing. A wrongly wired circuit or appliance may kill or maim.

Always use the correct size and type of cable for the job in hand and make sure that all work conforms to the IEE Regulations. Any good book on electricity will summarize these for you.

Always work back from the new circuit towards the live electricity source and don't make the final connection until you have double-checked all your work. Then switch off the electrical supply for the whole house before making the final connection. Plan your work so that you do this in daylight. Don't rush electrical work and don't take chances with electricity.

Always replace broken plugs and frayed cables before they become hazardous. If a plug feels warm after use, suspect a loose terminal.

Follow manufacturers' instructions when wiring new appliances. Don't omit earth connections unless the appliance is double-insulated (this will be stated or have the symbol, below right, shown on it). Do use an RCD with all garden equipment and power tools (see opposite). Do not overload sockets with adaptors.

Using a mains tester

With one finger on the metal button at the end of the handle, touch the blade point on to a live terminal or wire. If current is present, a neon lamp in the handle will glow. A built-in resistor prevents shocks.

Apart from the usual items found in the average householder's tool chest, the following specialized tools will make any electrical work easier.

Electrician's pliers
With insulated handles, these are used for cutting, bending and twisting heavy cable.

Side cutting nippers
For cutting flexes and conductors.

Neon mains tester
(See below, left).

Additional tools

For more ambitious work the following tools will be useful.

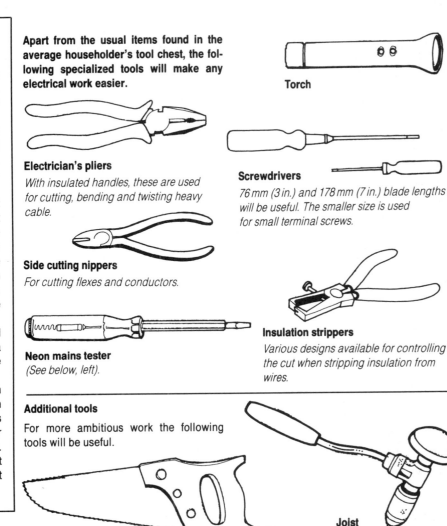

Torch

Screwdrivers
76 mm (3 in.) and 178 mm (7 in.) blade lengths will be useful. The smaller size is used for small terminal screws.

Insulation strippers
Various designs available for controlling the cut when stripping insulation from wires.

Floorboard saw
Floorboards can be sawn neatly over the joist with this tool.

Wrecking bar
For lifting floorboards and pulling nails.

Joist

Brace
Allows access between joists for drilling holes to run cables.

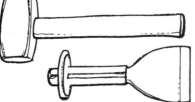

Club hammer and bolster chisel
For cutting channels in plaster to run cables.

Symbols found on appliances

Double insulated
The appliance does not require an earth conductor.

Earth
Connect the earth conductor to this terminal.

L **Live**
Connect the live conductor to this terminal.

N **Neutral**
Connect the neutral conductor to this terminal.

Wiring a plug

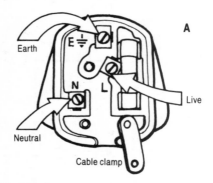

Earth

E ⏚

N   L

Neutral

Live

Cable clamp

A

B

C

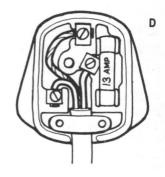

13 AMP

D

Remove the plug top and loosen one screw from the cable clamp **(A)**.

Slit the outer sheath lengthwise with a sharp knife. Peel it back and cut it off away from the wires **(B).** Use side cutters to cut the separate wires to length **(C)**.

Make sure that the outer sheath will be held securely by the cable clamp. Strip away only sufficient insulation from each wire to

pass through each terminal. Twist the ends and secure into their respective terminals and tighten the cable clamp **(D)**.

Note: some plugs have alternative cable clamping. Following the instructions supplied with the plug.

Check that each wire is secure and connected to the proper terminal, insert a correctly rated fuse and replace the plug top.

Remember! Green and yellow to earth terminal.
Brown to live terminal.
Blue to neutral terminal.

Fit the correct fuse: Red 3 amp, for appliances up to 720 watts; Brown 13 amp, otherwise.

13 AMP

HOOVER✦ MODEL   S1250
240v∼ 50 Hz 800w

BEAB
Approved

SER No S125060900327
✦ TRADE MARKS OF HOOVER plc
MADE BY HOOVER plc GREAT BRITAIN

Rating plate

This can usually be found on the back or the bottom of an appliance. Among other details, it will give the wattage for determining the correct fuse to be used in the plug.

Identifying conductors		
Live	Red	**Cable**
Earth	Bare	
Neutral	Black	
Live	Brown	**Flex**
Earth	Yellow/green	
Neutral	Blue	

Consumer unit fuses

Your consumer unit will contain one of the following types of fuse according to the date of its installation.

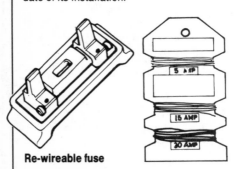

5 AMP

15 AMP

30 AMP

Re-wireable fuse

Three ratings: 5 amp for lighting circuits and 15 and 30 amp for power circuits.

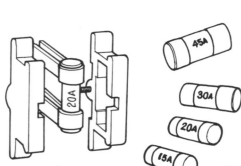

20A

45A

30A

20A

15A

6A

Cartridge fuse holder

Keep a stock of spare fuses.

20A

PUSH
OFF

Miniature circuit breaker (MCB)

Used in modern consumer units instead of fuses.

Cable and flex

Cable is used for fixed installations throughout the house. Flex is used to connect movable appliances to sockets, and light fittings to ceiling roses, etc. Cable and flex is designated by the cross-section of the copper conductors (wires). It is sold by the metre from most DIY outlets. For large jobs, 50 m and 100 m drums are available.

Cable	Type	Size	Fuse (at consumer unit)	Use
	Two-core and earth	6 mm²	30 amp	Cooker circuits up to 7.2 kW. Shower circuits up to 8.4 kW.
	Two-core and earth	2.5 mm²	30 amp	Ring circuits and spurs. Immersion heater circuits.
	Two-core and earth	1 mm²	5 amp	Lighting circuits.
	Three-core and earth	1 mm²	5 amp	Two-way switching in lighting circuits.

Flex	Type	Use
	Three-core circular, sheathed	All kinds of appliances
	Three-core, braided	Kettles and irons
	Three-core, heat-resistant	Immersion heaters and cookers
	Flat, twin-sheathed	Small light fittings
	Two-core, circular sheathed Also available in bright orange	Pendant lights. Double-insulated appliances. Double-insulated garden and workshop equipment
	Twin-bell wire	**Maximum** 50 volts. Use only for bell/chime pushes wired through a transformer.
	Co-axial cable 750 ohms. For TV and FM radio aerials	

Cable accessories

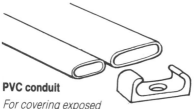

PVC conduit

For covering exposed cables or sinking in plaster. Available in 3 m lengths and the following sizes: 13 mm ($\frac{1}{2}$in.), 16 mm ($\frac{5}{8}$in.), 20 mm ($\frac{3}{4}$in.), 25 mm (1 in.) and 32 mm (1$\frac{1}{4}$in.).

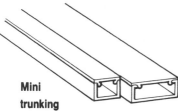

Mini trunking

Available in 3 m lengths and the following sizes: 16 ×16 mm ($\frac{5}{8}$in.), 16 ×25 mm ($\frac{5}{8}$×1 in.), 16 ×38 mm ($\frac{5}{8}$×1$\frac{1}{2}$in.) and 25 ×38 mm (1 ×1$\frac{1}{2}$in.).

Strip connector

Available as strips of twelve. Cut off as required. Ratings: 5 amp, 15 amp and 30 amp.

Cable clips

Available as flat for cable or round for flex and in various sizes. Select the correct size for the cable in use.

Sockets and FCUs

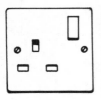

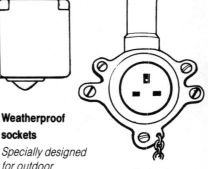

Flush and surface sockets

Sockets are available as flush or surface mounted, as switched or unswitched, and as singles or doubles.

Metal-clad surface socket

Used in situations like workshops.

Weatherproof sockets

Specially designed for outdoor siting.

Metal boxes

Used with flush sockets. Insert a rubber grommet in the knockout cable entry. Available as singles or doubles and shallow or deep.

Shaver supply socket

The only socket allowed in a bathroom. An overload device restricts the power so that only shavers can be operated.

Cavity wall box

Made in plastic, these boxes have spring-loaded lugs to grip the back face of the plasterboard.

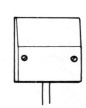
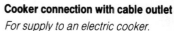

Cooker connection with cable outlet

For supply to an electric cooker.

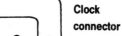

Clock connector

For connecting mains-operated clocks to the supply.

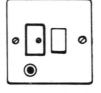

Fused connector units (FCUs)

These are used for connecting fixed appliances to the electricity supply. Various designs available.
Shown above are: fused, fused and switched with neon indicator, and fused and switched with flex outlet.

Trailing socket

Make up your own cable reel.

Blanking plate

For closing off redundant sockets.

Co-axial cable and fittings

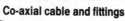

Co-axial plug

Strip the cable and fit the plug as shown.

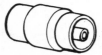

Co-axial connector

Connects cable between two plugs.

Co-axial socket

Neat outlet for TV or video aerial.

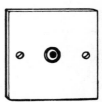

Switches and connectors

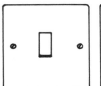

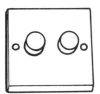
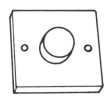
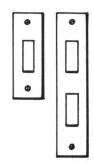

Switches

Usually flush fitting but also available for surface mounting.

Dimmer switches

Will progressively dim the room lights. Various designs available which replace the standard light switch.

Architrave switch

For use on door posts. Available both as flush and surface mounts.

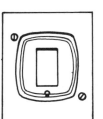

Metal boxes

Used behind flush switches to contain the live electrical parts.

Moulded plastic surface boxes

For surface mounting of switches.

Waterproof switches

For outside locations.

Cord pull switches

Safety light switches for bathrooms or cloakrooms. Higher rated versions for bathroom appliances.

Ceiling rose

For connecting pendant lights to the ceiling.

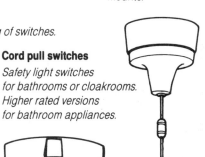

Batten lampholders

Straight and angled. For the direct mounting of lights.

Torpedo switch

Cord mounted switch with rocker operation.

Junction box

For spur connections to ring circuits or additional circuits for lighting. Check the rating when buying.

Lampholders

Made in plastic and brass and available in switched or unswitched versions.

Rubber flex connector

For connecting and extending flex to occasionally used appliances. Easily separated.

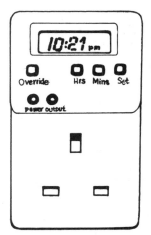

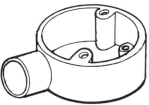

Besa box

Recessed into the wall for the direct mounting of wall lights.

Permanent flex connector

For permanently extending flex.

Timeswitch

Plugged into a socket, these can switch appliances on and off over a 24-hour period.

Lighting

Tungsten filament is by far the commonest form of lighting in the home (the familiar pear-shaped bulb). Fluorescent lighting is used mainly in offices and industrial situations, but has been adapted and miniaturized for the home. There are also fluorescent tubes in the form of bulbs now available (see below).

Tungsten filament bulbs are available in a vast range of shapes and sizes, some requiring special fittings. If the bulb you are replacing is anything out of the ordinary, it is best to take the old one along to the shop for proper replacement.

Use clear bulbs in enclosed fittings (they are brighter) and pearl where the bulb is exposed to the eye.

Holders are often marked with a maximum wattage. Don't exceed this or you may damage the fitting through overheating.

Bulb types (Tungsten filament)

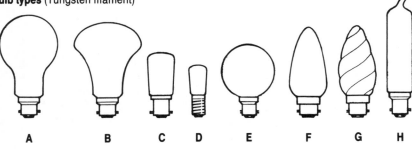
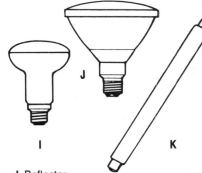

A. Standard pear shape
B. Mushroom
C. Pygmy
D. Appliance

E. Globe
F. Candle
G. Twisted candle
H. Pickwick

I. Reflector
J. PAR (Parabolic aluminized reflector)
K. Striplight

Fluorescent tubes

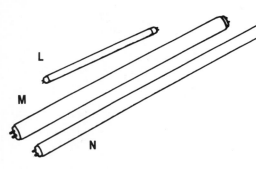
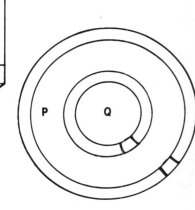

L. Mini
M. Standard 38 mm (1½ in.) diameter tube
N. Slimline 25 mm (1 in.) diameter tube

O. Fluorescent bulb SL
P. Circular 406 mm (16 in.)
Q. Small circular 305 mm (12 in.)

R. Low energy bulb.

Cap types
Tungsten filament caps

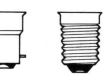

Bayonet cap (BC)

Edison screw (ES)

Small bayonet Cap (SBC)

Small edison screw (SES)

Fluorescent caps

Bi-pin

Double-ended tubular

Fluorescent tube starter

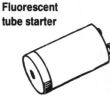

2 ratings;
4–80W
125W

Lighting

Tungsten filament bulbs

A guide to general availability is given below

Type	Cap				Pearl	Clear	Coloured	Crown silvered	Wattage	Use
	BC	ES	SBC	SES						
Basic pear	*	*			*	*	*	*	15,25,40,60, 75,100,150	Basic household lighting
Mushroom	*				*				40,60,100, 150	For shallow fittings. Gives a softer light.
Pygmy			*	*	Opal	*	*		15	Compact size. Use where space is limited.
Appliance			*	*		*	*		15,40	Appliances. Sewing machines, etc.
Globe	*	*					*		25,40,60, 100	Decorative bulbs for open display.
Candle	*		*	*		*	*		25,40,60	For wall lights and chandeliers.
Twisted candle	*		*		Silver light	*			25,40,60	For decorative reproduction candle fittings.
Pickwick	*		*		*		*		40	This candle bulb even has a wick. Used in flickering lamp fittings.
Reflector		*					*	*	40,60,75, 100,150	Special spot or flood holders.
PAR		*				*			80,100,150	Armoured glass for outside use.
Striplight		DET			Opal	*	*		30,60	For striplight fittings.

Fluorescent tubes

Type	Cap		White	Warm white	Daylight	Length mm	Wattage	Use
	Bi-pin	DET						
Standard 38 mm dia. (1½ in.)	*		*	*	*	600,900, 1200,1500, 1800,2400	20,30,40,50 75–85,125	Standard, large fluorescent tube. Mainly for workshop lighting.
Slimline 25 mm dia. (1 in.)	*		*	*	*	460,600,900 1200,1500	15,18,30,36, 50	Slimmer tube. For kitchens, etc.
Mini 15 mm dia. (⅝ in.)	Mini bi-pin		*				4,6,8,13	Worktop lighting in kitchens.
Circular 406 mm (16 in.)	4-contact			*			40,60	Decorative kitchen and bathroom lighting.
Small circular 305 mm (12 in.)	4-contact			*			32	Smaller version of the above.
Bulb SL	BC	ES		*			9,13,18	Long-life replacement for the tungsten filament bulb.*
Low energy bulb	BC adaptor			*			10,16,28	As above.

*Heavier than TF bulb.

Distribution

Domestic water distribution

The water supply pipe enters the house well below ground (about a metre deep) to avoid frost damage. There is usually a stop valve (tap) at the bottom of a large bore vertical pipe somewhere in front of the house. You will probably need a long-handled turnkey to turn it. It's as well to locate this at your convenience and check that it turns easily in case you should need it in an emeregency.

There is usually another stop valve low down somewhere inside the house, sometimes with a drain cock attached, to allow for complete drainage of the house cold water system.

A reservoir of cold water is held in a cistern in the loft or above the hot water cylinder. As hot water is drawn off it refills the hot water cylinder and is itself refilled by means of a ball valve directly from the main. This cistern may also serve some taps and toilet cisterns throughout the house, but at least one tap, usually in the kitchen, will come direct from the main. You can tell which taps come direct by the force of the water flow as mains water, from the Water Authority pumping station is under pressure and will eject much more forcibly from the tap.

Maintaining the house water supply in good order requires ensuring that ball valves are not sticking or leaking (overflow dripping), that all pipes in the loft are lagged against freezing, and that taps are not dripping. Pipe lagging and re-washering taps and ball valves are well within the capabilities of the average householder.

Household plumbing

Copper is by far the commonest material for central heating and domestic hot and cold water supply pipes, whilst plastic is used mainly for waste pipes. These are the only two materials likely to concern the DIY householder.

Copper pipe is commonly available in outside diameters of 15 mm, 22 mm and 28 mm and in three metre (10 ft) lengths.

It's easy to bend 15 mm pipe with an inexpensive bending spring: 22 mm is more difficult and for 28 mm it's best to use fittings to change direction.

To join metric pipe to old imperial copper pipe in an older house there are special adaptors available, so it's no problem to connect the two different systems. There is even an adaptor for joining old lead pipes to modern copper pipe, but as this requires a wiped joint it's best left to a plumber.

When fitting new sinks or basins always fit isolating valves (stop taps), so that tap washers can be changed without turning off the whole house supply.

Copper pipe sizes

Shown below are the three common household pipe sizes drawn actual size.

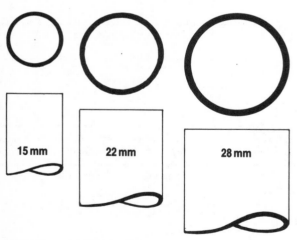

15 mm **22 mm** **28 mm**

Of the three sizes shown, 15 mm is used for hot and cold water supplies to basins, sinks, washing machines, etc. and central heating pipes to radiators. 22 mm is used for hot water supplies to baths, connections to hot water cylinders and main distribution pipes in central heating systems. The only applications likely in the home for 28 mm pipe are the main flow and return pipes to the boiler in the central heating system.

Materials for preparing and joining copper pipes and fittings

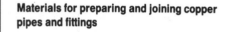

Wire wool
Used for cleaning the pipe ends prior to soldering.

Flux
Used on copper pipes and fittings before soldering. It helps the solder run freely.

Jointing paste
Used on compression joints to make a watertight seal.

Solder
Plumbers solder is 3 mm dia. solid wire solder in $\frac{1}{4}$ kg reels.

PTFE tape
A very thin conformable plastic tape which is wrapped around the threads of fittings like radiator valves, and boiler and hot water cylinder connections.

Tools

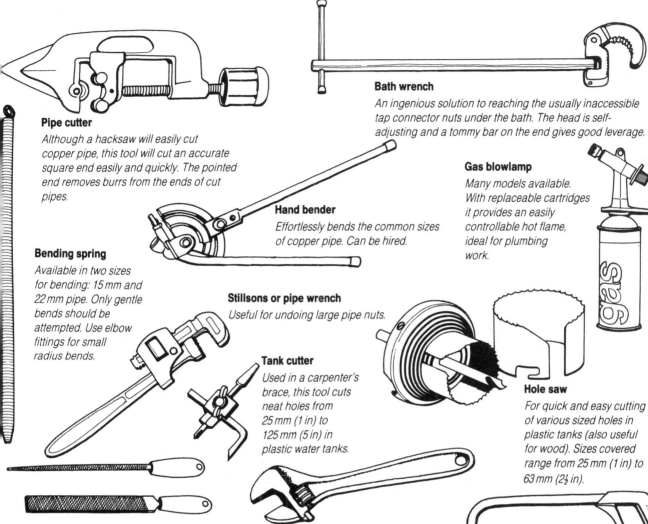

Pipe cutter

Although a hacksaw will easily cut copper pipe, this tool will cut an accurate square end easily and quickly. The pointed end removes burrs from the ends of cut pipes.

Bath wrench

An ingenious solution to reaching the usually inaccessible tap connector nuts under the bath. The head is self-adjusting and a tommy bar on the end gives good leverage.

Gas blowlamp

Many models available. With replaceable cartridges it provides an easily controllable hot flame, ideal for plumbing work.

Hand bender

Effortlessly bends the common sizes of copper pipe. Can be hired.

Bending spring

Available in two sizes for bending: 15 mm and 22 mm pipe. Only gentle bends should be attempted. Use elbow fittings for small radius bends.

Stillsons or pipe wrench

Useful for undoing large pipe nuts.

Tank cutter

Used in a carpenter's brace, this tool cuts neat holes from 25 mm (1 in) to 125 mm (5 in) in plastic water tanks.

Hole saw

For quick and easy cutting of various sized holes in plastic tanks (also useful for wood). Sizes covered range from 25 mm (1 in) to 63 mm ($2\frac{1}{2}$ in).

Files

Two are required. A flat file for filing cut pipe ends square and a small round file for cleaning off the burrs from the inside.

Adjustable spanner

Ideally two are needed to manipulate compression fittings without marking the surface. Minimum openings required are 35 mm ($1\frac{3}{8}$ in) to cover 22 mm fittings.

Hacksaws

Use a hacksaw with a fine blade to cut pipe if you're lacking a proper pipe cutter.

Wire pipe brush

Inexpensive tool which quickly cleans the insides of capillary and end feed fittings before soldering.

Basin wrench

A useful tool for undoing the tap nuts under a basin when access is limited.

Smaller version of the above. Useful for sawing off pipes in situ if access is limited.

Joist brace

Special tool for drilling holes in joists to run pipes under floorboards. Joists are too closely spaced to allow an electric drill or normal brace to operate.

Spade bit

Used in an electric drill to make a hole in the floorboards for a pipe to run through.

Pipe fittings

Straight coupling
For extending straight lengths of pipe.

Equal tee
For branching off at right angles.

Reducing tee (End reduced)
For joining various sizes of pipe at right angles.

Reducing tee (Branch reduced)

Elbow
For making a right-angled turn.

Reducing tee (Both ends reduced)

Reducing tee (One end and branch reduced)

Swept tee
Used for assisting the flow of water in a certain direction.

Reducer
For joining one size of pipe to another. Various sizes available.

Adaptor (Metric × Imperial)
Available as 15 mm × $\frac{1}{2}$ in, 22 mm × $\frac{3}{4}$ in and 28 mm × 1 in. For joining old imperial pipe to modern metric pipe.

Stop end
For sealing the ends of pipes. Useful as a temporary measure when working on a job which must be left for a while.

Straight swivel tap connector
Available as 15 mm × $\frac{1}{2}$ in and 22 mm × $\frac{3}{4}$ in. For connecting taps to pipework.

Air bleed valve
Can be fitted in the high parts of a closed circuit such as pumped hot water in a central heating system.

Tank connector
Specifically designed for connecting to plastic water tanks. Don't forget the washers.

Bent swivel tap connector
Available as 15 mm × $\frac{1}{2}$ in and 22 mm × $\frac{3}{4}$ in. For connecting taps to pipework.

Male iron socket adaptor
For connections to boilers and hot water cylinders via an adaptor.

Female iron socket adaptor
Inside thread for connections to boilers and hot water cylinders via an adaptor.

Three basic designs of fitting are available for joining copper pipe:

1. End feed fittings. Straight-sided, simple and cheap. Solder must be added when making the joint.

2. Capillary solder ring fittings. These have an integral ring of solder formed during manufacture. When heat is applied the solder 'creeps' out of the ring and fills the gap between the pipe and the fitting. Neat and permanent.

3. Compression fittings. More expensive and bulkier—but no heat is required to join

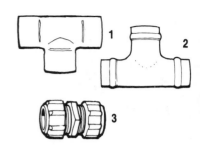

these, just spanners. The joint can be undone and remade. Bear in mind that it can be difficult to manipulate spanners in a restricted space.

Copper pipe connectors

Below are some of the commonly available joints for copper pipe. The basic shapes are all available in 15 mm and 22 mm sizes, but larger sizes may only be stocked by specialist plumbing merchants. Most are available as end feed, capillary and compression fittings.

Note. Bath taps are designated $\frac{3}{4}$ in and basin and sink taps $\frac{1}{2}$ in.

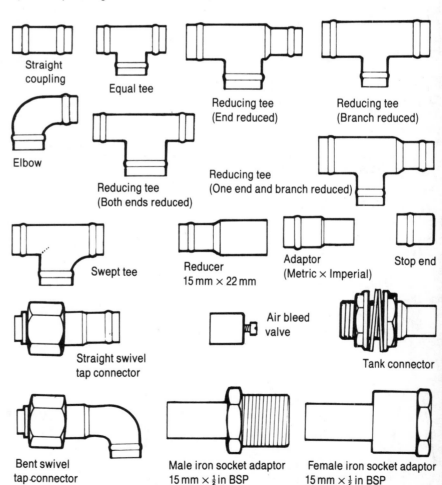

Straight coupling

Equal tee

Reducing tee (End reduced)

Reducing tee (Branch reduced)

Elbow

Reducing tee (Both ends reduced)

Reducing tee (One end and branch reduced)

Swept tee

Reducer 15 mm × 22 mm

Adaptor (Metric × Imperial)

Stop end

Straight swivel tap connector

Air bleed valve

Tank connector

Bent swivel tap connector

Male iron socket adaptor 15 mm × $\frac{1}{2}$ in BSP

Female iron socket adaptor 15 mm × $\frac{1}{2}$ in BSP

Pipe fittings

Gate valve

A metal gate operates inside the body and there is no replaceable washer, so it is often used to isolate hot water cylinders and feed and expansion tanks.

Stop valve

Often used to control the whole house water supply. When fitting make sure the arrow stamped on the body matches the water flow.

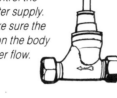

Flexible copper pipe

Ideal for making those difficult tap connections when fitting a new bath, basin or sink. One end is a tap connecter and the other will accept solder or compression fittings. Available as 15 mm or 22 mm.

Wall plate elbow

Useful for fitting a tap to a wall.

Washing machine valve

Specially designed miniature valves which connect directly between 15 mm pipe and the flexible washing machine hose. They come with two tap heads so you can fit the colour to match the water supply. Red for hot and blue for cold.

135° elbow

Use where a gentle bend is required and pipe bending is not possible.

Drain cock

For draining down systems. This one is for fitting above a stop valve. Another version fits a pipe end. A standard garden hose fits the outlet.

JOINING PIPE

Capillary solder fitting

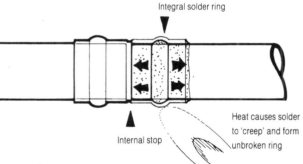

Integral solder ring

Heat causes solder to 'creep' and form unbroken ring

Internal stop

Compression fitting

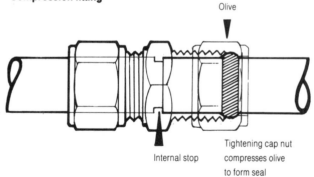

Olive

Internal stop

Tightening cap nut compresses olive to form seal

Pipe preparation

To use both capillary and compression fittings, first make sure that the pipe ends are square by using a flat file if necessary. Clean off inner burrs with a small round or half-round file and clean the pipe end with wire wool.

Capillary fittings

Make the pipe end bright and clean, well beyond the fitting length, by using clean wire wool. Clean the inside and the end of the fitting in a similar way. Do not touch the areas that have been cleaned.

Apply a liberal coating of flux around the pipe end and inside the fitting, using a small, clean brush. Push the pipes into the fitting up to the internal stop. Heat the fitting with a blowlamp until the solder runs and forms an unbroken seal around the end of the fitting, adding extra solder if necessary. Note. All the outlets on a capillary fitting must be joined at the same time, as fittings heat quickly and the solder will run from any open end.

Check all round the fitting using a small mirror to see the back. Wipe off excess flux. Turn on the water and check for leaks.

Compression fittings

Undo and remove the cap nut and olive. Slide these up the pipe away from the cut end. Position the olive at its approximate final position and smear the olive and the pipe end with jointing paste. Push the pipe fully home against the stop inside the fitting, secure the cap nut in position and, using two adjustable spanners—one to hold the centre nut and the other the cap nut—tighten the fitting down.

Note. Do not apply extreme force as it will distort the pipe and olive.

Screwed fittings

Fittings which are commonly connected to boilers and hot water cylinders have a tapered thread. Before tightening the fitting and so completing the seal, the threads must first be wrapped with three or four turns of PTFE tape to make a watertight seal. If you are connecting up to an established boiler or cylinder clean out the threads on the old fitting with a wire brush.

Hot water cylinders

The hot water cylinder is the large, domed, copper container which usually sits in the airing cupboard. There are various systems according to the age of your installation. The oldest is the direct system, where heating pipes of large bore, 28 mm (1 in), run from a back boiler behind an open fire or room heater. The heated water rises into the hot water cylinder, displacing the cold water which sinks to the back boiler to be heated in turn. The actual water thus heated is drawn off directly for domestic purposes.

In an indirect system, now the most common, the heated water circulates in a separate heat exchanger, inside the hot water cylinder, and passes its heat to the water inside the main cylinder, which is then drawn off as required.

A combined cylinder package system is often fitted in flats, where space is limited. In this a small cold water cistern sits atop the hot water cylinder. The hot water cylinder has screwed bosses for horizontal installation of immersion heaters.

A third type is known as the self-priming cylinder and, although basically a direct system, the primary and secondary water supplies are kept separate by an ingenious design which causes a large air bubble to form between them.

A lot of hot water cylinders now come with a thick coating of expanded polystyrene on the outside to reduce heat loss. This is a much more efficient way of insulating a cylinder than the old loose quilted jacket and should be used wherever possible.

Cylinder sizes and shapes

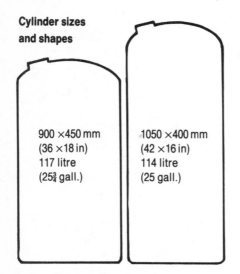

900 ×450 mm
(36 ×18 in)
117 litre
(25¾ gall.)

1050 ×400 mm
(42 ×16 in)
114 litre
(25 gall.)

Standard sizes are shown here. The tall, thin cylinder is very useful for a narrow cupboard.

Typical indirect cylinder layout

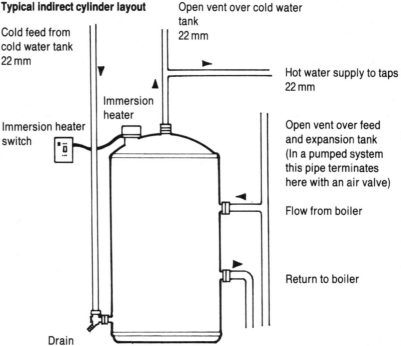

Cold feed from cold water tank
22 mm

Open vent over cold water tank
22 mm

Immersion heater switch

Immersion heater

Hot water supply to taps
22 mm

Open vent over feed and expansion tank
(In a pumped system this pipe terminates here with an air valve)

Flow from boiler

Return to boiler

Drain

Immersion heater

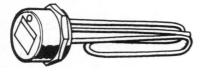

This is screwed into the large opening usually on the top of the cylinder. The central rod contains a thermostatic sensor which switches the heater on when the water temperature in the cylinder drops below a certain level. Usually rated at 3 kW, there are different types for different purposes. Connect it to the switch using a heat resisting flex. (See page 53).

Immersion heater spanner

These large spanners are available for hire or can be purchased.

Blanking plug

If fitting a new cylinder and an immersion heater is not required, blank off the hole with one of these.

Adjusting the thermostat

Turn the heater off and remove the cover. You will usually find a large adjusting screw with marks around the periphery. These usually coincide with water temperatures of 60°C (140°F), 71°C (160°F) and 82°C (180°F). Water should not be so hot as to be dangerous to the users, particularly old people and children.

Taps

Anatomy of a pillar tap with fittings

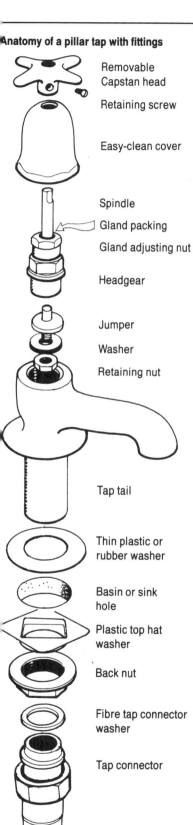

- Removable Capstan head
- Retaining screw
- Easy-clean cover
- Spindle
- Gland packing
- Gland adjusting nut
- Headgear
- Jumper
- Washer
- Retaining nut
- Tap tail
- Thin plastic or rubber washer
- Basin or sink hole
- Plastic top hat washer
- Back nut
- Fibre tap connector washer
- Tap connector

There is an enormous variety of taps now available, but they all fit into one of the categories shown here. For changing washers it is necessary to shut off the water supply to that tap, except in the case of the Supatap.

Pillar tap

Bib tap

Supatap

Shrouded-head tap

Bath/Shower mixer tap

Sink mixer

Pillar tap

This is the straightfoward basic design of household tap, usually chrome-plated on brass.

Supatap

A revolutionary design of kitchen tap with an integral anti-splash device in the nozzle.

Bib tap

This type of tap is useful for outdoor siting and is connected via a wall plate elbow (see page 61). Some versions have a hose union outlet for the easy connection of a garden hose.

Shrouded-head tap

This type of tap is very common nowadays, usually with a decorative acrylic head.

Bath/shower mixer tap

A simple adjustment of a plunger or lever diverts the mixed water to either the taps or the shower head.

Sink mixer

Various patterns available with long swinging arms to deliver the water over either basin of a double sink.

Washers

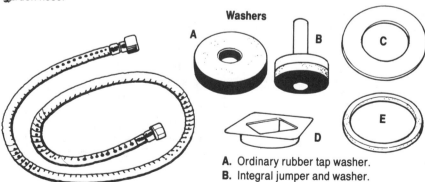

A. Ordinary rubber tap washer.
B. Integral jumper and washer.
C. Thin polythene washer for use between tap body and basin.
D. Plastic top hat washer which goes under the bath or basin before securing the tap with a back nut.
E. Fibre washer fitted to a tap connecter before securing it to the tap tail.

Replacement shower hose

Shower hoses can eventually fail as the inner rubber pipe wears and springs a leak. Be sure to use the rubber washers supplied when making the new connection.

Cisterns and ball valves

Cold water storage cisterns

In older houses the cold water storage cistern will most likely be a square galvanized tank. Although long-lasting, the increased use of copper pipes since these were installed caused electrolytic action to take place in the cistern, with slow but steady corrosion as the result.

Modern cisterns, made from various plastics, are light and easy to handle and are available in all shapes and sizes.

The recommended capacity for a cold water storage capacity is 227 litres (50 gall.). Smaller sizes are available for feed and expansion tanks for central heating.

Some flexible plastic cisterns will fold in on themselves for easy access through a loft trapdoor. A plastic cistern requires a solid flat base, something to consider when replacing a metal one that had stood on open joists.

The base of the new cistern should be at a minimum of 1.5 m (5 ft) above the rose of a gravity fed shower. Some cisterns have a metal reinforcing plate fitted to support the ball valve. If this is not the case the inlet hole should be at about 50 mm (2 in) below the rim. The overflow or warning pipe should be at about 50 mm below the inlet. The outlet pipes should be about 50 mm above the base.

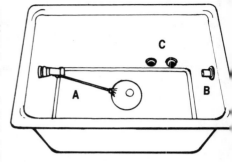

Typical cistern installation
A. Ball valve and inlet pipe.
B. Overflow or warning pipe.
C. Outlet pipes.

Ball valves

There are several different designs of ball valves in use and what you have may depend on the date of your house and of the plumbing installation.

The older types were made of brass and they went on working without any attention for years. The newer ones are made of plastic and by comparison seem flimsy.

Both types will need attention from time to time, mainly washer replacement in the case of the former and plunger replacement for the latter.

There are high pressure valves for connection directly from the mains and low pressure for where the supply comes from a storage cistern. Diaphragm valves are adjustable to both pressures.

On ball valves with brass arms, the correct water level is achieved by gently bending the ball arm. Plastic valves have a screw and locknut adjustment where the arm contacts the valve.

Croydon valve
These are possibly the oldest type and can be recognized by their vertical plunger and twin water jets. Washer replacement is similar to the Portsmouth type.

Ball valve floats

Plastic floats are readily available to replace copper ones that have become perforated.

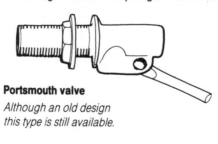

Portsmouth valve
Although an old design this type is still available.

Diaphragm valve
The modern type of ball valve. Unscrew the knurled cap to gain access to the rubber replaceable diaphragm.

Washer replacement on a Portsmouth ball valve

Turn off the water supply and remove the split pin securing the ball arm. If a cap is fitted, unscrew this and ease out the brass plunger using a screwdriver in the slot underneath. Close inspection should reveal where the washer cap is screwed to the plunger. Hold the plunger in a vice and, using pliers, unscrew the cap. The rubber washer can now be prised out with a small screwdriver and replaced.

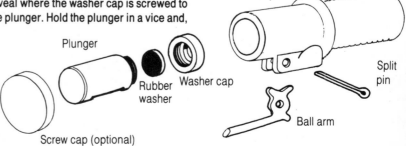

WCs

There are various patterns of WC pans and cisterns. Two basic shapes of pan are the 'P' trap and the 'S' trap and if you're replacing a WC you need to know which type will fit your existing waste pipe. 'P' traps are designed for where the pipe passes through an outer wall into the soil pipe. 'S' traps connect to a pipe passing through the floor.

The oldest type of cistern is the high-level bell cistern, made from cast iron. Low-level cisterns are divided into two types. The older type has a bent pipe connecting the cistern to the pan, while the other sits directly on the pan and is known as 'close-coupled'. Close-coupled pans can be wash-down, single-trap syphonic or double-trap syphonic.

If an older low-level cistern requires repeated pumping of the handle to flush, it probably needs a new diaphragm (see diagram). Although polythene diaphragms are cheap and readily available, the entire mechanism inside the cistern must be removed in order to replace it.

Toilet pan traps

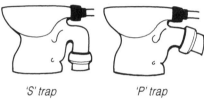

'S' trap   *'P' trap*

Replacement flushpipes

All shapes available, even for high-level cisterns. Take the old pipe with you to match up.

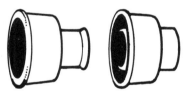

Flushpipe connectors

Flexible plastic connectors to replace leaky rubber ones.

Replacement toilet seats

Various colours available in plastic as well as solid wood. Toilet seat fittings are also available on their own.

Multikwik connector

For connecting a new toilet to an existing cast-iron soil pipe Multikwik connectors are the answer. Some of the available shapes are shown here. The old cast-iron spigot may need to be sawn off to get the new toilet in position against the wall – use an angle grinder for this.

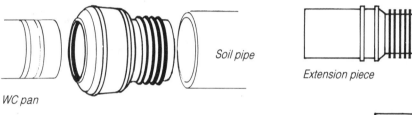

WC pan   *Soil pipe*   *Extension piece*

Multikwik connector

A watertight joint is created by the multiple plastic and rubber flanges on both the inside of the soil pipe and the outside of the pan spigot.

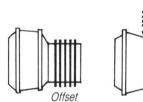

Offset   *Bend*

Inside a direct action toilet cistern

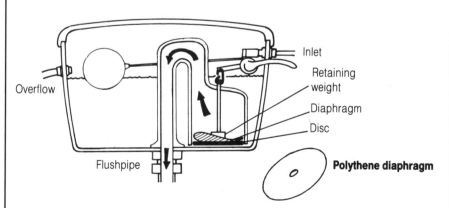

Overflow

Inlet

Retaining weight

Diaphragm

Disc

Flushpipe

Polythene diaphragm

When the handle is operated it forces the flexible diaphragm, supported by a perforated disc, to the top of the chamber, pushing the water before it. This creates a vacuum at the bottom of the chamber, drawing up the remaining water. The ball valve falls and allows the water to be replenished via the inlet pipe. The weight and disc fall to the bottom of the chamber, with the diaphragm bending up to allow the free flow of water through the holes in the disc. When the pre-determined water level is reached the ball valve shuts off the supply.

Plastic pipes

For waste pipes throughout the house, modern plastics (mainly uPVC [unplasticised polyvinyl chloride] and polypropylene) are now the popular choice. Solvent-welded plastic pipes can also be used for hot and cold water and central heating, but for some reason haven't been widely accepted for this particular use.

Sizes

For baths, showers and sinks use 38 mm (1½ in) waste pipes and for hand basins 32 mm (1¼ in) pipes. These are still sold in 1½ in and 1¼ in sizes and not their metric equivalents.

For overflows from cisterns use 22 mm (¾ in).

For washing machines and dishwashers follow the manufacturers' installation recommendations.

Note. Different systems from different manufacturers, although nominally of the same size, are not usually interchangeable. The best bet is to check what your local supplier has most of and stick to that brand.

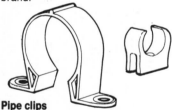

Pipe clips

Pipe clips should be used at regular intervals on both horizontal and vertical pipe runs. Types are available for both copper and plastic pipes.

Tip

Ease the fitting of pipes into push-fit joints by smearing the ends with washing-up liquid.

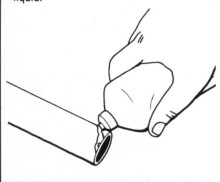

Fittings

Pipe fittings are usually in ABS (acrylonitrile butadiene styrene) and come in prepacks with printed instructions. Fittings for plastic pipes are available in similar basic configurations to those for joining copper pipes (see page 60), so it's easy to plan your pipe runs.

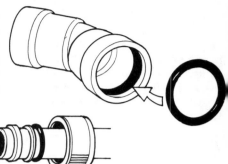

Traps

The purpose of waste traps is to seal the installation, bath, sink, etc., from foul air rising from the drain. This is achieved by a reservoir of water being 'trapped' in the bends. A waste trap also allows one to gain access to the waste pipes in the event of a blockage and serves the additional purpose of collecting small items of jewellery that have slipped from one's hands.

Some basins, sinks, baths and shower trays come complete with the waste and plug fitting and it's just a case of measuring up the supplied parts and matching up the required plastic plumbing. Make sure you've listed everything including pipe clips before buying.

Trap types

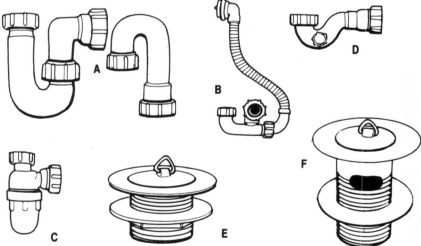

A. Two-way sink and basin trap
The basic basin trap which screws directly to the basin waste (**F**). Two outlets are supplied for either vertical or horizontal pipe runs.

B. Bath trap with integral overflow
This trap screws directly to the bath waste (**E**), with the overflow pipe connected to the overflow hole.

C. Bottle trap
Bottle traps for basins and sinks are less convoluted than **A** and provide a neater appearance where the pipework is on view.

D. Shallow bath/shower trap
A very useful design for modern baths which are set lower than older types. This will fit where the standard trap may not.

E. Bath waste
These are usually chrome-plated on brass, although moulded plastic ones are also available.

F. Basin/sink waste
As **E**.

Drainage

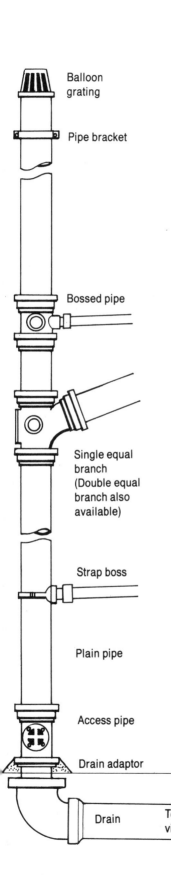

Balloon grating

Pipe bracket

Bossed pipe

Single equal branch (Double equal branch also available)

Strap boss

Plain pipe

Access pipe

Drain adaptor

Drain

To main sewer via inspection chambers

Drainage

Since the 1960s all main drainage has been via the single stack system. Prior to this only WCs were connected to the soil stack; bath, basin and sink wastes were taken out through the wall to discharge over open gullies, a legacy from the Victorian era. In modern plumbing they all discharge into a single stack.

What you have will depend on the age of your house and whether your drainage system has been updated since it was built. If you have the older type, any additional sinks or showers, etc. can simply be discharged as previously over the gully. But if you are adding a new WC where there was none before you may have to update the whole of your drainage system to a single stack, as there is no way you can break into a cast-iron soil pipe.

Plastic soil pipe is available in 2 and 3 m lengths (6 ft 6 in and 10 ft) and in 110 mm (4 in) diameter. For connections, push-fit

with a rubber seal is the commonest, but solvent weld is also available.

Fittings

There is a wide range of fittings similar in function to the smaller plastic waste fittings described opposite. See what your local supplier has and try to obtain a leaflet to aid planning.

Note

Don't confuse rainwater downpipes with soil pipes. They are two separate systems. In modern houses rainwater is dispersed into a convenient soakaway or storm drain, but in some older properties it was often discharged into the sewer.

Regulations

There are strict regulations concerning single stack systems, as WC and kitchen waste pass through the same pipe. Therefore you must contact your local building inspector before making any alterations.

Drainage inspection chamber

Every house has at least one inspection chamber. The one shown is the older type, with glazed earthenware pipes and channels. Typically this would be the last one before the main sewer and is usually found in the front garden, sometimes with an air vent poking up nearby.

The rodding eye can be removed for unblocking the lower pipe with drain rods should this ever become necessary. Occasional inspection and sluicing with water will help keep these trouble free.

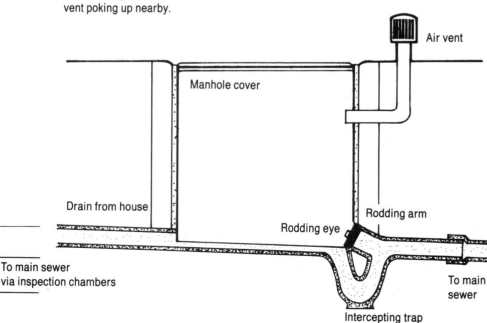

Manhole cover

Air vent

Drain from house

Rodding arm

Rodding eye

To main sewer

Intercepting trap

Central heating

A brief description of central heating is included here to help you understand how it works and the types and use of various controls.

How central heating works

The small feed and expansion tank (**A**), usually sited in the loft, is connected by a ball valve to the rising main water supply. This maintains the water level in the boiler (**B**). It also allows for expansion of the heated water to run over the expansion pipe (**C**) back into the tank. In practice the water in the system will find its own level and will only overflow or need replenishing in extreme situations, or when the system has been altered. This pipe may also have a safety valve (**D**) fitted near the boiler.

The radiator circuit

The pump (**E**) pushes the heated water through the pipes to the various radiators (**F**)—only one is shown—where it passes via the handwheel valve (**G**) through the radiator waterways and out via the lock-shield valve (**H**) to the return pipe and back to the boiler. The handwheel valve can be used to temporarily shut off a radiator. The lockshield valve is covered with a plastic cap and is adjusted by the installer to balance each radiator in turn to restrict the flow and allow radiators further from the boiler their share of heat. A small key is used on the vent at the top of one end of each radiator to allow trapped air to escape. After heating the radiators, the water flows back under the pressure of the pump, along the return pipe to the boiler to be re-heated and re-circulated.

The cylinder circuit

The hot water is heated indirectly – unlike old systems where the actual water from the back boiler was drawn off and used for baths, etc.—which means it passes through a coil inside the cylinder (**I**) and gives up its heat to the main body of water in the cylinder which can then be drawn off. This means that anti-corrosive chemicals can be added to the central heating system to protect radiators without contaminating the hot water.

Gravity system

In system 1 the cylinder circuit is circulated by gravity through large-bore pipes. Hot water is lighter than cold, so a natural circulation is set in motion when water is heated.

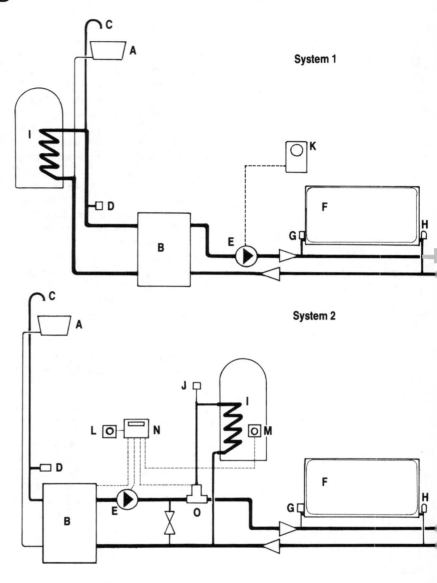

System 1

System 2

In system 2 the cylinder circuit is pumped through small-bore pipes for a more rapid heat-up of hot water. An air bleed valve (**J**) is fitted at the highest part of this circuit to vent trapped air.

Controls

System 1 shows a very basic design consisting of only a timeswitch (**K**) to control the system. Temperature is controlled by the boiler thermostat.

System 2 shows a more sophisticated set-up, with radiators controlled by a room thermostat (**L**) and hot water controlled by a cylinder thermostat (**M**). These are both controlled, in turn, by a programmer (**N**), as is the diverter valve (**O**) which directs the flow to either the radiators or cylinder or

both according to needs. Programmers can be set to switch heating/hot water on and off twice in every 24 hours. There are many systems and controls, this shows but two of them.

Fuel

Electricity is not covered here as the only type of central heating powered by this fuel is supplied by storage radiators, which are usually fitted by the local Electricity Board.

Gas

The most popular fuel for central heating. No storage problems, clean and available nearly everywhere, with the largest range of boilers. If you are not connected to mains gas there are systems which use propane

Central heating

gas delivered by tanker and stored in a tank sited outside.

Solid fuel
Can be used in either room heaters, open fires with high-output back boilers or free-standing boilers.

Oil
Once very popular because it was very cheap, it is still useful in rural areas where gas is not available. Oil boilers are usually sited in outhouses or special boiler rooms. Room for a large storage tank with tanker

access is also required.
Wood
If you do not live in a smokeless zone and have access to a plentiful supply of dry wood there are some specially designed wood-fired boilers available.

Faults in central heating systems
Problems with central heating systems, whenever they occur, always seem to happen at the most inconvenient time and for this reason alone it's well worth having a maintenance contract with a reliable company who will come quickly to repair

your system.
Modern boilers are complex pieces of engineering, and nowadays rely increasingly on electronics as well. A good heating contractor will hold the parts for your boiler in stock and will be able to replace faulty

parts without trouble.
Boiler manufacturers often offer their own service contracts and these are well worth taking up. Otherwise look in the Yellow Pages.

Problem	Possible cause	Action
Nothing working	Boiler failure Timeswitch or programmer altered or faulty System fuse or boiler fuse blown Wiring disconnected Boiler dry	Call service engineer Adjust timeswitch or programmer Call service engineer Replace fuse and check cause Check wiring or call service engineer Refill system and check for leaks
Boiler working but no heat	Pump faulty Thermostat turned down	Test and replace pump if necessary Adjust thermostat
Noisy pump	Air or sediment in pump	With pump turned off, open bleed screw on top of pump body to release air Open drain at lowest part of system and allow clean water to run through
Pump won't start	Pump jammed or failed	Turn pump rotor using screwdriver slot Renew pump
One radiator cold	Thermostatic radiator valve turned down or air-lock in pipe	Adjust valve Turn off all radiators except the problem one and turn the pump to its maximum to clear air lock
Radiator cold at top, warm at bottom	Air in radiator	Bleed radiator (see next page)
Radiator hot at top, cold at bottom	Corrosive sludge in radiator	Drain and remove radiator and flush through with a hosepipe.
Some radiators very hot, some cool	System needs balancing	Call service engineer or adjust lockshield valves throughout
Radiator leaking along bottom	Corroded radiator	Replace radiator with one of the same size
Leaks from around compression joints (common)	Loose compression fitting	Tighten fitting with spanners (see page 61)
Leaks from soldered joints (rare)		Drain system and remake joint (see page 61)
Overflow running in feed and expansion tank	Faulty ball valve Water level set too high Water pumping over from expansion pipe	Renew washer or ball-valve Bend ball valve arm to proper water level Adjust pump or have system checked

Central heating 2

A. Pump

A good quality, reliable pump is absolutely essential, as this is possibly the hardest-working part of the system, switching on and off thousands of times during a heating season. Ideally it should be set between isolating valves (A1) to allow future removal without draining the system.

Controls

B. Programmer

Programmers vary from fairly basic to highly sophisticated devices packed with microchips to control a multitude of functions. Study manufacturers' literature to see which suits your proposed needs.
This is the 'brain' of the system and tells the boiler, pump and diverter/zone valves when and how to operate.

C. Room thermostat

This is set by the user to the desired house temperature. It is connected through the programmer to switch off the boiler or divert the zone valve when that temperature is achieved and switch on again when the temperature falls.

D. Cylinder thermostat

This is strapped to the hot water cylinder, in contact with the metal surface, and is set by the user to the water temperature required. Connected via the programmer, it will switch on the boiler and operate diverter/zone valves when the water temperature falls and off when the predetermined temperature is reached.

E. Zones valves/diverter valves

Available in various configurations these are plumbed-in to the primary pipework and connected to the programmer. A small motor, mounted on top, will open or close different waterways to control the heating water to either the radiator circuit, cylinder circuit, upstairs or downstairs circuit, according to the system layout.
Study manufacturers' literature to assess which is suitable for your needs.

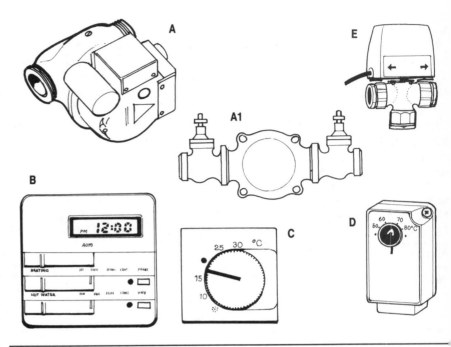

Boilers

Boilers fall naturally into several different types and some are applicable to all fuels.

Freestanding oil boiler (1)

Freestanding boilers can be fired by gas, oil and solid fuel and range in size from compact types that fit neatly into kitchen worktops to the relatively large high-output oil boilers for siting in a boiler room.

Wall-hung gas boiler (2)

These can be quite small and light and can be sited in other rooms as well as kitchens.

Solid fuel room heater (3)

Also available as gas- and wood-burning types, these fully-enclosed boilers can be either freestanding or designed to be fitted into a fireplace.

Open fires

Specially designed open coal fires have deep ashpits and high-output back boilers to power a small central heating system.

Aga-type boilers

Popular for country kitchens, this old design has been upgraded to heat radiators and burn any fuel.

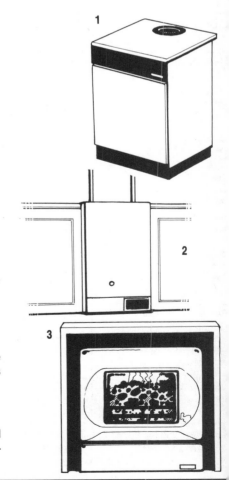

Central heating 2

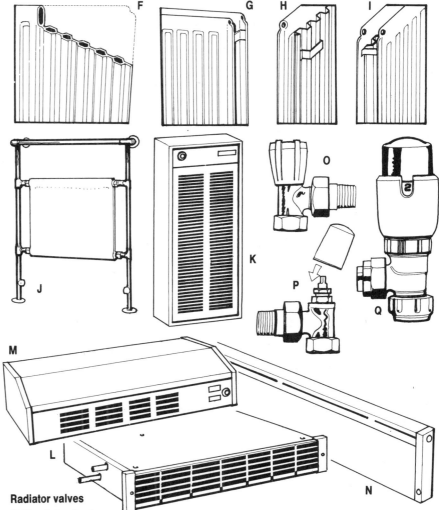

Radiators

Radiators are the business end of the heating system and there are various types to suit different situations.

F. Single panel radiator

Simple pressed-steel inexpensive radiator.

G. Double panel radiator

Two singles constructed together to give out approximately two-thirds more heat than a similar-sized single, but without taking up any more space.

H. Single panel convector

With fins welded to the back to increase the radiating surface, this design increases output by about a quarter without any significant increase in fuel cost.

I. Double panel convector

This has fins welded between the two panels to increase output further.

All the above are available in a vast range of sizes and outputs to heat whatever space is required.

J. Towel radiator

Designed for bathrooms and cloakrooms. Constructed of large-bore, chromium-plated pipes offering a convenient surface for hanging towels, it may or may not include a small heating panel.

Convector radiators

Considerably more expensive than panel radiators by virtue of their more elaborate construction, they include a fan for more rapid heat-up. They are useful where space is lacking and for special applications. A limited range of sizes is available.

K. Standard convector

Available in different heights and widths with a decorative wooden casing.

L. Kickspace convector

Very useful in kitchens where space is at a premium this is set into the plinth at the bottom of standard kitchen units and blows out heat where it's most appreciated—at foot level.

M. Downdraught convector

Similarly useful in kitchens, this is set above a door and blows down warm air.

N. Skirting radiator

Fitted in place of the skirting boards, it provides the most unobtrusive radiator system available.

Radiator valves

O. Handwheel valve

This is fitted where the flow pipe joins the radiator and can be used to turn the radiator on or off.

P. Lockshield valve

This is connected where the return pipe leaves the radiator and is used to control the flow of water through the radiator. It is adjusted by the installer and should not be interfered with unless the radiator is to be removed or the system needs balancing.

Q. Thermostatic radiator valve

This is a self-actuating valve fitted in place of the normal radiator valve. It senses the surrounding air temperature and closes off the valve progressively, opening it up to a predetermined setting when the temperature falls. It's very useful in rooms which get temporarily overheated, such as kitchens during cooking.

Tip

Bleeding a radiator

Carefully open the vent at the top of the radiator until you hear hissing and gurgling sounds. With a cloth held ready, close the vent with the key immediately water starts to spurt out.

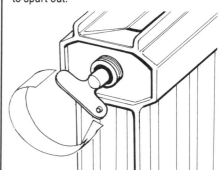

Nails

Type	Finish	Use	Sizes (mm)
Round wire nail	Bright Galvanized	For all general-purpose carpentry. Use galvanized for fencing and outdoor work.	20, 25, 40, 50, 65
Lost-head wire nail	Bright	Use where appearance matters as the head is not exposed.	25, 40, 50, 65
Oval wire nail	Bright	Being oval in cross-section, this type is less likely to split the wood.	25, 30, 40, 50
Cut nail	Steel	Mainly used for floorboards where the square tip lessens the risk of splitting.	50, 60, 65
Cut clasp nail	Steel	For rough fixing including into masonry.	50, 60, 65
Masonry nail	Zinc-plated	Use when fixing into concrete, brickwork or masonry.	20, 25, 32, 38, 50 55, 65, 75, 90, 100
Lath nail	Galvanized	Mainly used for roofing, but useful for all outdoor work.	25, 30, 40, 50
Sprung head nail	Galvanized	For fixing corrugated sheeting.	65
Corrugated fastener	Bright	Used for rough wood-frame construction.	12, 16, 20
Staple	Bright Galvanized	For fixing wires to fences.	15, 20, 25, 30, 40
Plasterboard nail	Galvanized	Jagged shank and countersunk head. High resistance to pulling out.	25, 30, 40
Pipe nail	Galvanized	For fixing cast-iron down-pipes to walls	40, 50
Panel pin	Bright	All kinds of light fixings, especially where the head is to be punched down.	13, 16, 20, 25, 30 40, 50

Nails

Type	Finish	Use	Sizes (mm)
Hardboard nail	Copper Bright	Copper version will not discolour hardboard and paint.	20, 25, 30, 38
Tack	Blued Galvanized	Used for carpet, underfelt and hidden upholstery fixing.	20, 25
Glazing sprig	Steel	Holds glass panes secure in window frames. Is hidden by putty.	12, 20
Clout nail	Galvanized	For roof tiling and fixing roofing felt.	13, 20, 25
Cut copper slate nail / Copper wire slate nail	Copper	Used for fixing slates. Will not rust.	30, 40, 45
Upholstery nail (Decorative)	Brass Bronze Chrome	Exposed upholstery fixings.	12
Gimp pin	Zinc-plated	For fixing braid in upholstery.	9, 13, 25, 30, 40

Claw hammer

The claw is used to lever out the nail once it has been knocked back from the other side of the timber.

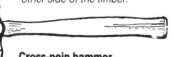

Cross-pein hammer

Use the pein (the narrow part of the head) to start small nails.

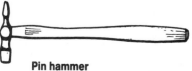

Pin hammer

Use for small nails and pins.

Nail sets or punches

For punching nail heads below the surface. They are available in a range of point sizes.

Pincers

For pulling nails. Some types have a tack lifter incorporated in the handle.

Tack lifter

For levering out tacks, small nails and pins.

Fixing and removing nails

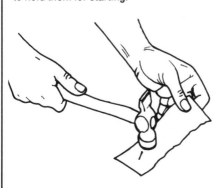

Hammer wedges

When a new hammer shaft is fitted, these are driven into the top of the shaft to tighten the head.

Tip

Push small pins through a piece of thin card to hold them for starting.

Screws

Wood screws are manufactured in steel, brass, aluminium and stainless steel. The finishes available are: bright zinc plate, sherardized, nickel plate, chromium plate, brass plate and black japanned. The exposed heads of steel screws should be painted over with metal primer when used in conditions liable to damp, otherwise use one of the non-corroding variety.

Aluminium screws are useful for cedar wood as they don't stain. Use brass screws for decorative brass fittings, however, as brass screws are expensive and liable to break if forced, it is important to drill the correct pilot holes. It is a good idea to drive a steel screw of the same size into the wood first.

Measuring screws

Screws are measured in length as shown at 'A' for the different head types.
Gauge is the diameter of the shank (the unthreaded part) as shown at 'B'. Common gauges are shown below left.

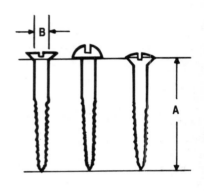

Screw sizes and clearance holes					
Gauge No.	4	6	8	10	12
Clearance Hole for shank	3 mm ($\frac{1}{8}$ in.)	4 mm ($\frac{5}{32}$ in.)	5 mm ($\frac{3}{16}$ in.)	5 mm ($\frac{3}{16}$ in.)	6 mm ($\frac{1}{4}$ in.)
Hardwood Pilot hole	2 mm ($\frac{5}{64}$ in.)	2 mm ($\frac{5}{64}$ in.)	3 mm ($\frac{1}{8}$ in.)	3 mm ($\frac{1}{8}$ in.)	4 mm ($\frac{5}{32}$ in.)
Softwood Pilot hole	Bradawl	Bradawl	2 mm ($\frac{5}{64}$ in.)	2 mm ($\frac{5}{64}$ in.)	3 mm ($\frac{1}{8}$ in.)

Screw sizes

Gauge	Generally available sizes
No 4	10 mm ($\frac{3}{8}$ in.), 13 mm ($\frac{1}{2}$ in.), 19 mm ($\frac{3}{4}$ in.), 25 mm (1 in.).
No 6	13 mm ($\frac{1}{2}$ in.), 19 mm ($\frac{3}{4}$ in.), 25 mm (1 in.), 32 mm ($1\frac{1}{4}$ in.) 38 mm ($1\frac{1}{2}$ in.), 50 mm (2 in.).
No 8	13 mm ($\frac{1}{2}$ in.), 19 mm ($\frac{3}{4}$ in.), 25 mm (1 in.), 32 mm ($1\frac{1}{4}$ in.), 38 mm ($1\frac{1}{2}$ in.), 50 mm (2 in.), 63 mm ($2\frac{1}{2}$ in.).
No 10	19 mm ($\frac{3}{4}$ in.), 25 mm (1 in.), 32 mm ($1\frac{1}{4}$ in.), 38 mm ($1\frac{1}{2}$ in.), 50 mm (2 in.), 75 mm (3 in.), 100 mm (4 in.).
No 12	38 mm ($1\frac{1}{2}$ in.), 50 mm (2 in.), 75 mm (3 in.), 100 mm (4 in.).

Screw length

Where possible, the length of the screw should be approximately three times the thickness of the wood being secured.

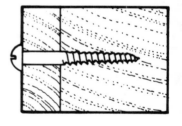

Tip

Dip steel screws in grease or Vaseline before screwing home especially in outdoor locations. This makes future removal much easier.

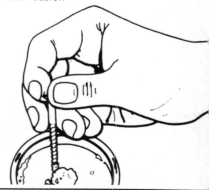

Screw caps and cups

A. Surface screw cup
Made in brass this is used to strengthen thin material or to avoid countersinking.
B. Brass insert screw cup
Lies flush with the surface of the wood. A very neat, strong fixing.
C. Plastic dome cap
The screw is set into a pre-drilled 10 mm hole and the cap is a push fit in the hole. Available in white and various browns to

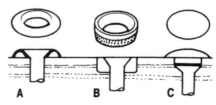

match melamine-faced chipboard. Other types of screw covers are available but they are generally matched to a particular screw design.

Screwdrivers

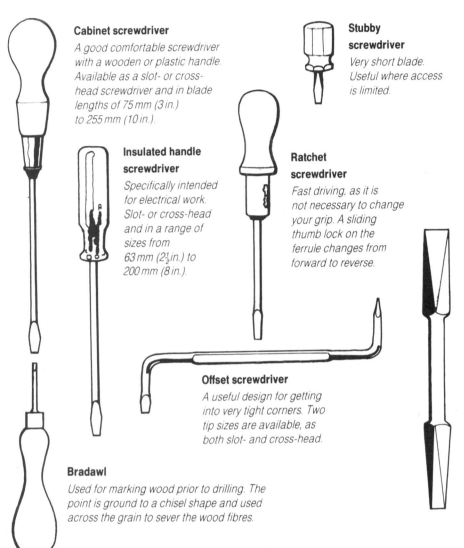

Cabinet screwdriver

A good comfortable screwdriver with a wooden or plastic handle. Available as a slot- or cross-head screwdriver and in blade lengths of 75 mm (3 in.) to 255 mm (10 in.).

Stubby screwdriver

Very short blade. Useful where access is limited.

Spiral ratchet screwdriver

Patented design screwdriver with several useful features. Pushing down on the top handle, whilst steadying the chuck with the other hand, transforms the downward motion into turning force. A change of the thumb lock reverses the action for withdrawing screws. Screwdriver and drill bits of various sizes make this a very versatile tool.

Insulated handle screwdriver

Specifically intended for electrical work. Slot- or cross-head and in a range of sizes from 63 mm (2½ in.) to 200 mm (8 in.).

Ratchet screwdriver

Fast driving, as it is not necessary to change your grip. A sliding thumb lock on the ferrule changes from forward to reverse.

Brace screwdriver bit

These bits exert tremendous torque when used in a brace and can shift the most stubborn screw.

Offset screwdriver

A useful design for getting into very tight corners. Two tip sizes are available, as both slot- and cross-head.

Bradawl

Used for marking wood prior to drilling. The point is ground to a chisel shape and used across the grain to sever the wood fibres.

Watchmaker's screwdrivers

Available in sets for intricate work.

Screw head types

A   **B**   **C**   **D**   **E**

A. Clutch head
Can be screwed in but not out. Used for security items like door locks.

B. Cross head
Three types: Phillips, Supadriv and Pozidriv. Phillips heads are becoming less common, but you will still come across them.

C. Slot
The standard screw head. Use the correct size of screwdriver matched to the head of the screw to avoid damaging the wood, the screw or the screwdriver.

D. Dome head
Decorative screws with a chrome- or brass-finished dome which scews into the head. Used mainly for mirrors.

E. Coach screw
Heavy-duty screw with a square head for fixing into rough timber.

Rechargeable electric screwdriver

A powered screwdriver which takes the hard work out of driving screws, especially if you have a lot of assembly work in hand. Supplied with several bit sizes, both cross and slot.

Hinges

Types of hinge

There's an infinite variety of hinges to suit all sorts of applications and choosing the right one requires a certain amount of care. Butt hinges are the commonest type and are usually sandwiched between the edge of the door and the door frame so that when the door is closed only the knuckle of the hinge shows. Butt hinges require careful fitting and ideally a tapered recess should be cut to avoid binding.

Of all the other types of hinge the one which the homeowner is most likely to come across is the concealed hinge, which is found on the inside of kitchen cabinets. The practical advantage of this hinge is that the door can be adjusted vertically, horizontally and inwards and outwards, very useful where a series of doors needs to be aligned.

This type usually requires a blind hole of 26 or 35 mm (1 or 1⅜ in) diameter which can only be cut with a special drill bit used in a pillar drill.

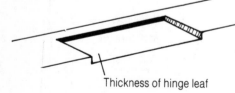

Butt hinge

The commonest type of hinge. Made in brass, steel and nylon. Vast range of sizes from 25 mm (1 in) to 100 mm (4 in) long. Large, brass decorative types are useful for quality entrance doors.

Thickness of hinge leaf

Tapered recess for butt hinge

Ideally a butt hinge should be set into a tapered recess and the knuckle of the hinge should protrude by about the thickness of the hinge at the knuckle.

Piano hinge

Narrow butt hinge in continuous lengths up to 2 m (6 ft). Saw to length required with a hacksaw.

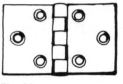

Flap hinge

Wide leaves on this hinge make it especially suitable for drop flaps on tables and desks.

Counter hinge

Used for table tops and counter flaps. The dovetail shape gives added security recessed into a hanging flap.

Snake hinge

A decorative design based on antique originals.

Cylinder hinge

Fitted into pre-drilled holes, the cantilevered arm allows the door to open well clear of the cabinet. Folding doors can be constructed using cylinder hinges.

Rising butt hinge

Very useful because as the door opens it rises to clear the carpet. Additionally the door can be lifted straight off the hinges for decoration etc. These hinges need very careful fitting. Make sure you buy either left-hand or right-hand pairs according to which side of the door is hinged.

Flush hinge

Simple to fit as no recess is required, just the clearance between the door and the frame.

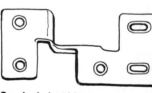

Cranked pivot hinge

Easier to fit than the standard pivot hinge.

Pivot hinge

Fitted to the top and bottom of doors and therefore invisible when the door is closed.

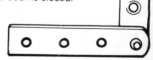

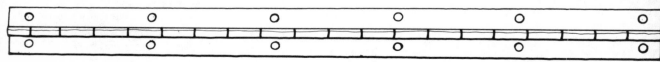

Hinges

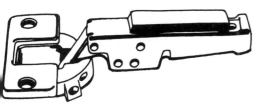

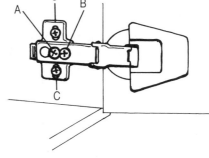

Concealed hinge

Now almost universally fitted to kitchen cabinets. Most types require a large blind hole for fitting on the back of the door. Besides being invisible when the door is shut, the range of adjustment is unique to this hinge.

Hinge sinker

A drill bit specially designed for fitting concealed hinges. Used with a power drill in a stand, the shoulder prevents the bit cutting through the door completely. Two sizes are available for 26 and 35 mm (1 and 1⅜ in) holes.

Blanking plug

If you need to change the hinges of a kitchen door from one side to the other, these plastic push-fit plugs will hide the ugly hole.

Adjustment of concealed hinges

Lateral adjustment
Slacken screw A and adjust screw B until sideways adjustment is correct. Re-tighten Screw A.

Vertical adjustment
Loosen screws C on both hinges and adjust door up or down as necessary.

Inward and outward adjustment
Loosen screw A and slide door in or out. Note. Hinges may vary. Experiment to find which screw does what.

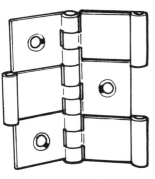

Screen hinge

A three-section hinge which moves in both directions. Use it for multi-panel doors and screens.

Single and double cranked hinges

The advantage of a cranked hinge is that the door opens within the width of the cabinet – useful where space is limited, such as cupboards in recesses.

Single and double spring hinges

A strong spring returns the door to the closed position. The double hinge is for saloon style doors which swing both ways. The hinge returns the doors to the centre position.

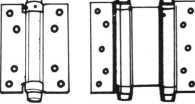

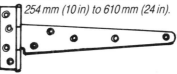

Strap hinge

Black japanned steel hinge used on shed doors. Sizes from 254 mm (10 in) to 610 mm (24 in).

Reversible hinge

Heavy duty hinge for garage doors and large gates. Sizes from 406 mm (16 in) to 610 mm (24 in).

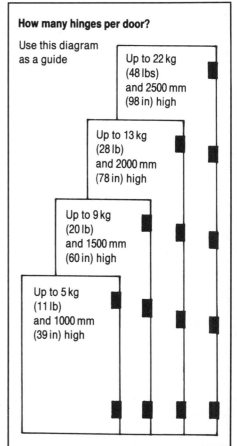

How many hinges per door?

Use this diagram as a guide

Up to 22 kg (48 lbs) and 2500 mm (98 in) high

Up to 13 kg (28 lb) and 2000 mm (78 in) high

Up to 9 kg (20 lb) and 1500 mm (60 in) high

Up to 5 kg (11 lb) and 1000 mm (39 in) high

Wall fixings

Before you drill into any wall you will need to know what lies beneath the surface. All being well it will be something solid enough to support your proposed fixing, but it could also be electric cables or water pipes. An indication of where cables lie can be gained by looking at the position of wall lights or sockets: the cables to them normally run vertically, although this is not always the case. Obvious signs of water pipes will be nearby taps etc. An electronic stud and cable finder is a worthwhile investment. This will beep when it detects cables or pipes. Some types will even detect solid timber frames in a partition wall—very useful for getting a really strong fixing.

Identifying wall construction

The first step is to ascertain whether the wall is solid or hollow, which is usually revealed by tapping. A modern construction—plasterboard on adhesive dabs—can sound hollow, but as there are lightweight blocks just behind the plasterboard it can be treated as a solid wall. This will become clear as soon as you drill into it.

The area directly above windows and doors is rather different, as wall openings are supported by strong lintels knows as RSJs. These can be made of steel or reinforced concrete and are difficult to drill into.

Choosing wall fixings

Use these pages to identify the type of wall fixing most suitable to your needs. Fixings require a correctly-sized hole, drilled to the proper depth, with a masonry drill. The drill size is usually indicated on the pack.

Electronic stud and cable finder (See text)

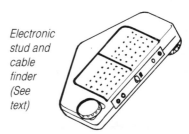

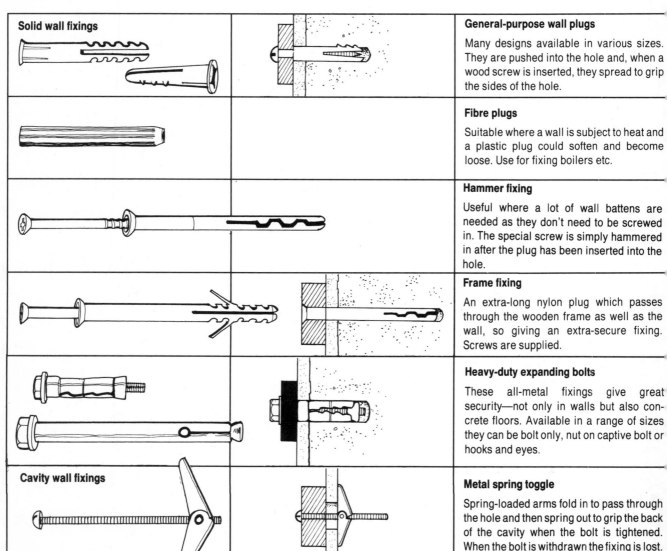

Solid wall fixings

General-purpose wall plugs

Many designs available in various sizes. They are pushed into the hole and, when a wood screw is inserted, they spread to grip the sides of the hole.

Fibre plugs

Suitable where a wall is subject to heat and a plastic plug could soften and become loose. Use for fixing boilers etc.

Hammer fixing

Useful where a lot of wall battens are needed as they don't need to be screwed in. The special screw is simply hammered in after the plug has been inserted into the hole.

Frame fixing

An extra-long nylon plug which passes through the wooden frame as well as the wall, so giving an extra-secure fixing. Screws are supplied.

Heavy-duty expanding bolts

These all-metal fixings give great security—not only in walls but also concrete floors. Available in a range of sizes they can be bolt only, nut on captive bolt or hooks and eyes.

Cavity wall fixings

Metal spring toggle

Spring-loaded arms fold in to pass through the hole and then spring out to grip the back of the cavity when the bolt is tightened. When the bolt is withdrawn the fixing is lost.

Wall fixings

Cavity wall fixings

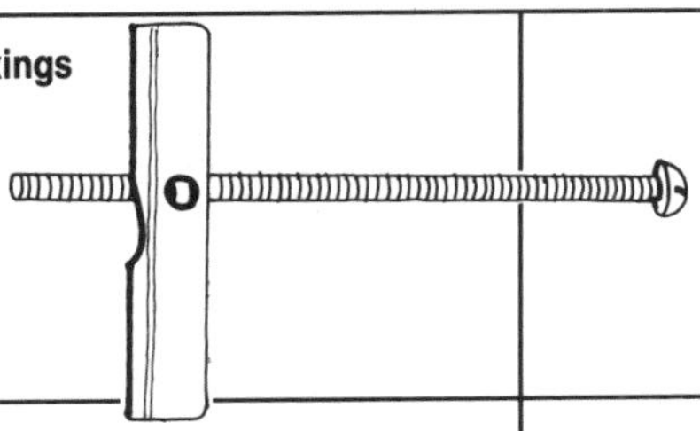

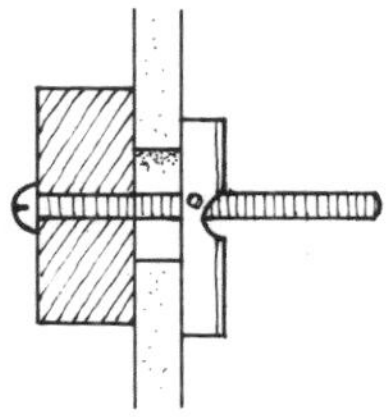

Metal drop toggle

The U-shaped bar is aligned with the bolt for insertion through the hole and then drops at right angles to secure the fixing. The fixing is lost when the bolt is withdrawn.

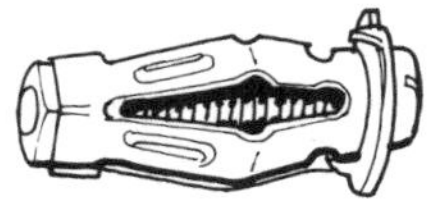

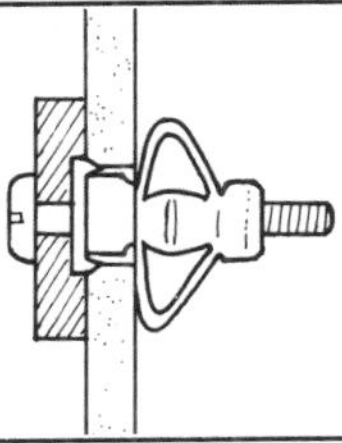

Heavy duty fixing

An all-metal plug that deforms on the inside when the bolt is tightened. Prongs on the head-washer bite into the plasterboard to lock the fixing and stop it turning. Bolt can be removed without loss of fixing.

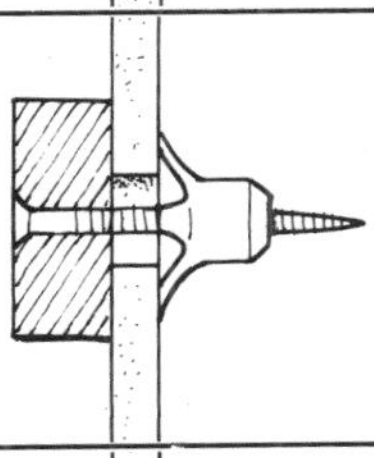

Nylon anchor dowel

The petals spring out to grip the back of the cavity after the dowel is pushed through a hole with a wood screw attached. Useful where the cavity is narrow. The fixing is lost when the screw is withdrawn.

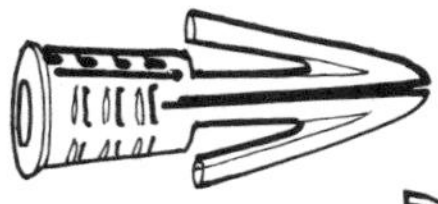

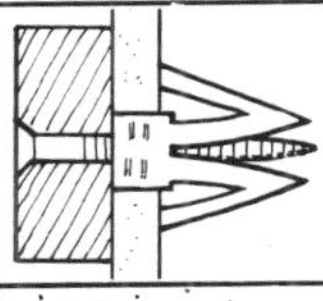

Winged nylon plug

Lugs spring out to grip the back surface whilst the body of the plug fits neatly into the hole, allowing for re-use.

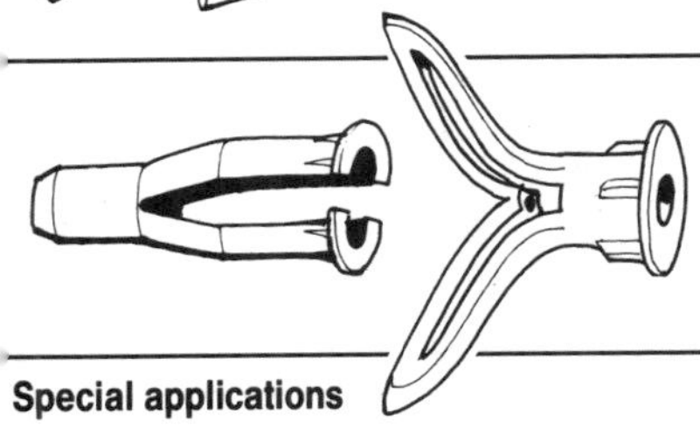

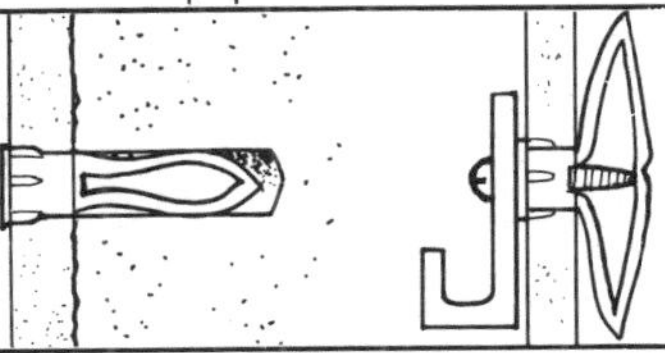

Dual-purpose nylon plugs

These will either spread in a solid wall or deform behind a cavity, giving a strong fixing in either.

Special applications

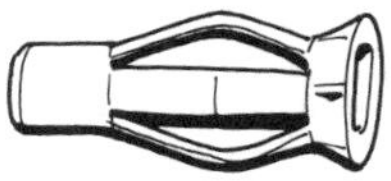

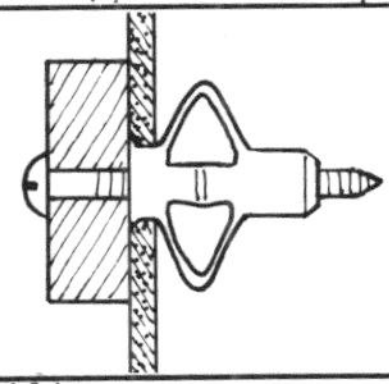

Light-duty door fixings

Specially designed for hardboard and plywood-surfaced hollow doors, these nylon plugs deform on the inside when tightened with a wood screw.

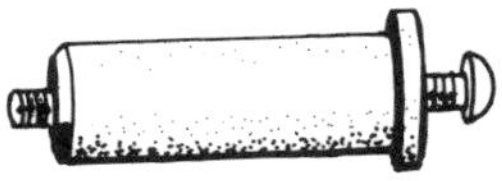

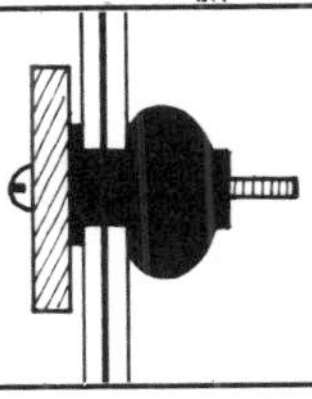

Anti-vibration fixing

Especially good for joining sheet metal, this rubber plug has a nut moulded into the back. When the bolt is tightened the plug deforms and locks the panels together. The bolt can be removed without loss of fixing.

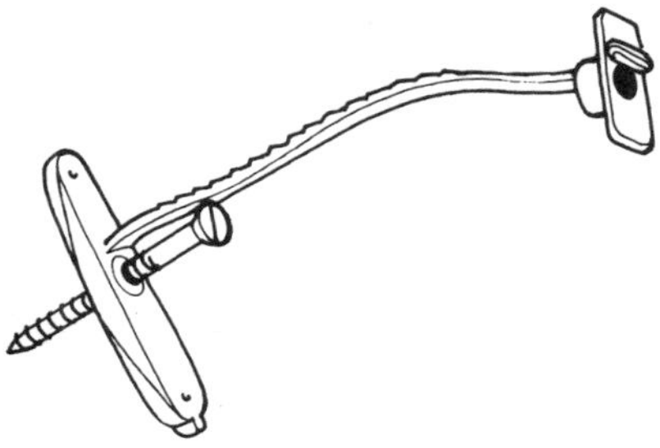

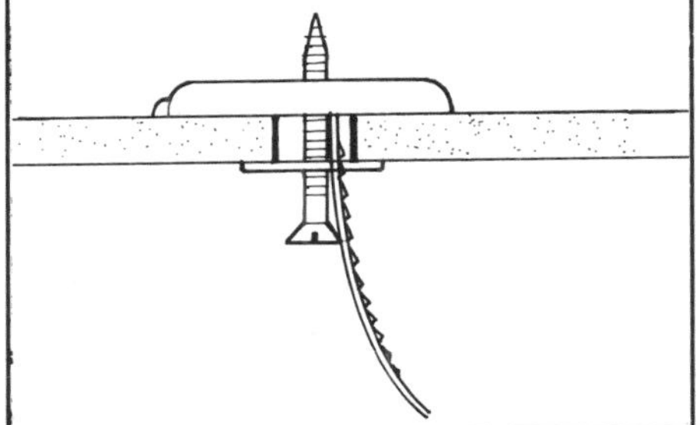

Ceiling toggle

The nylon bar, with the strap attached, is pushed into the ceiling cavity and the outer collar placed in the hole. The locking strap is then pulled up tight to position the spreader bar and the screw is inserted. The strap can be cut off flush. The locking strap ensures that the fixing remains in position whenever the screw is withdrawn.

Adhesives

The range of modern adhesives is complex and constantly being added to. Always read the manufacturer's information on the pack before buying so as to ascertain that a particular adhesive is suitable for your purpose.

Some adhesives give off noxious fumes. Always use these in a well-ventilated area. Some are inflammable. Don't smoke or use with naked flames.

Although setting times for some adhesives can be quick, it's always wise to wait about 24 hours before bringing the articles back into use.

Don't stick handles back onto cups, teapots or saucepans. A failure of the joint could be dangerous.

Type	Use/Properties	Gap filling?	Water-proof?	Cleaning off*	Pack	Bond
GENERAL PURPOSE						
Cyanoacrylate adhesive (Super glue)	For small intricate repairs. Expensive. Rigid plastics/Metal/Jewellery/Ceramics/China/Porcelain/Rubber/Leather	No	No	Acetone	Tiny tube	Immediate
2 pack Multibond	As above.	No	Yes	Acetone	Small bottle Small tube	Immediate
Acrylic adhesive	As above. Will stick oily surfaces.	Yes	Yes	Soapy Water	Twin pack	5 minutes
Epoxy resin	When all else fails use this. Metal/Wood/Rigid plastics/China/Ceramics	Yes	Yes	Meths	Twin pack	48 hours
CONTACT						
Latex rubber	Fabrics/Carpets/Leather/Cloth/Soft toys Paper/Card	No	Yes	Water	Plastic pot	Almost immediate
Synthetic rubber	Laminates to wood/Light fixings for metals and painted surfaces/Cork tiles	Some	Yes	—	Tubes and tins	Immediate
Synthetic rubber (adjustable)	Thixotropic (non-drip) version of the above. Allows for repositioning of materials.	Some	Yes	Tins	Slight time delay	
PAPER						
Starch Dextrine	Easy-to-use paper adhesive.	No	No	Water	Pots	Few minutes
Spray adhesive (Tri-chloroethane)	For mounting paper and card. Can be peeled and repositioned.	No	No	Lighter fuel	Aerosol cans	Immediate
WOODWORKING						
Animal and fish glues (Scotch glue)	Traditional, pot-boiled woodworking glue. Still available through specialist woodworker suppliers.	No	No	Water	Pearls and solid chunks	24 hours
Urea-formaldehyde	Two-pack woodworking adhesive.	Yes	Yes	—	Two-pack	6 hours
Resin	Dry powder mixed with cold water for use.	Some	Yes	—	Tins	6 hours
PVA (Polyvinyl acetate)	White liquid, ready-to-use glue. For wood and other dry porous materials.	No	No	Water	Plastic applicator	24 hours

Adhesives

pe	Use/Properties	Gap filling?	Water-proof?	Cleaning off*	Pack	Bond
ECIALIZED						
C adhesive	For repairing flexible PVC, like beach balls etc. Can melt through very thin PVC.	No	Yes	—	Small tube	Almost immediate
stic solvent VC	For joining plastic pipes	No	Yes	—	Tubes	Few minutes
lystyrene ment	For plastic kits and toys.	Yes	Yes	—	Small tube	Few minutes
llulose stes	Wallpapers of all types.	Some	No	Water	Dry powder in bags	12 hours
panded lystyrene ment	Ceiling tiles and coving.	Yes	Yes	Water	Larger tubes and tubs	1 hour
ass bond ethacrylate ter	For joining or fixing to clear glass only. Cures by ultra-violet light.	Some	Yes	—	Tiny tube	24 hours
tex rubber oring hesive	For bonding carpets and other materials to concrete floors. Vinyl tiles/Cork tiles Linoleum/Felt.	Some	Yes	Water	Tins	Few hours
ofing-felt hesive	For bonding roofing-felt to wooden or previously felted roofs.	Yes	Yes	—	Tins	1 hour
ramic tile ment	For fixing ceramic wall tiles.	Yes	Yes	Water	Dry powder in tubs	12 hours
ramic floor- adhesive	For floor tiles and shower trays.	Yes	Yes	Water	Read-mixed	12 hours
ll panel hesive	Applied by cartridge from a caulking gun. For fixing wall panels, skirtings and acoustic tiles directly to walls.	Yes	Yes	—	C30 cartridge	Few minutes

Preparation

A glued joint relies on the surface areas being a good fit and on cleanliness. Small broken ceramics or rigid plastics are best repaired as soon as possible after breakage, while the surfaces are still clean. Dry the parts and place them together to check the fit. Mark a line across the joined areas if the break is complicated and hold the parts with masking tape while the glue sets. Wood joints should be well-made and close-fitting, but not so tight that the glue is forced out or the joint will be weak.

Flexible, bendy plastics (Polypropylene and polyethylene) like washing up bowls and buckets are virtually impossible to glue. Likewise breakages to rigid plastics where the load is high and the gluing area small, as on the nose joint of spectacles.

*Refers to uncured adhesive. Once dry, adhesive may have to be cut away.

Electric glue gun

Sticks of glue are heated and applied through a nozzle neatly and cleanly. Rapid bonding takes place as the glue cools. Mainly used for woodwork, but adhesive sticks are also available for general purpose gluing.

Pest and fungus damage

Serious problems

Among the most serious problems affecting the householder and requiring immediate professional help the following should be included:

Rats (1) (1a Rat droppings shown actual size)

Any sighting of a rat—a large brown rodent with a body length of 200–255 mm (8–10 in) long—should be dealt with promptly as they are disease-carriers and potentially dangerous. Considering that the rat population of this country is equivalent to the human population, you are quite likely to see one from time to time.

Contact your local environmental health officer for advice. Small terrier-type dogs will kill rats quickly and efficiently but the usual recourse is to poison bait. This can be bought from hardware stores, but as it is poisonous to household pets as well, the manufacturers' instructions must be followed implicitly.

Good hygiene will deter rats—never leave meat or fish around and never put these on the garden compost heap or out for birds. Don't leave household refuse in flimsy plastic sacks, put it in a secure bin.

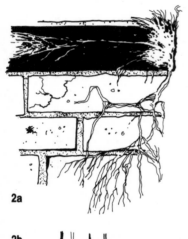

Dry rot (2a Early stage) (2b Fruiting bodies)

This, without doubt, is the most serious fungus problem that can affect a house, not to be confused with wet rot which can be overcome relatively easily. Dry rot will only occur in damp, unventilated places. The spores (microscopic airborne reproductive cells) are present almost everywhere but they can only start to grow when conditions are right, although once established they can send out moisture seeking filaments to continue their inexorable onward growth.

Eradication consists of the removal and burning of infected timbers well beyond their apparent spread, the scorching of nearby brickwork to kill any spores and the injecting of powerful fungicides into sound timber—so, it is not a DIY job.

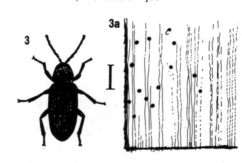

Woodworm (3 Adult beetle) (3a Typical timber damage shown actual size)

There are several species of wood-boring beetle, but the only one likely to affect the average home is the Furniture Beetle or Woodworm. It's the larvae (grubs) not the adult beetles that do the damage, spending several years tunnelling and weakening structural timbers and only betraying their presence by making the characteristic round holes as they exit, as adults to mate and lay further eggs that will continue the attack.

You are unlikely to recognize the adult beetle as it is quite small and only appears on windows etc, in July and August. To prevent woodworm attack treat all unpainted timbers by spraying (you can hire the equipment) or brushing with woodworm killer (see page 16). It is a messy job but once done will protect for years.

Some houses may have old woodworm infestations that have been treated and have died out, but it's possible to see if the insect is still active by looking for the frass (sticky sawdust lighter than the surface timber) near the exit holes. However a serious infestation requires professional treatment.

Two other serious faults affecting houses are settlement and rising damp. Settlement can occur when the soil dries excessively and this can be made worse by large trees too near the house taking up moisture through their roots. This condition is indicated by continuous cracks running vertically through brickwork. Don't confuse this with cracked rendering or the shrinkage of plaster in new homes. This is fairly normal as all houses move to a certain extent. Call a qualified surveyor if you are worried.

Rising damp is caused by the damp proof course breaking down or being covered by debris or soil. Damp from the ground seeps upward, spoiling decorations and causing mould growth. Don't confuse this with bad condensation which is caused by a lack of ventilation and low or no heating in rooms. If you suspect your damp proof course is faulty call in a specialist.

Pest and fungus damage

Lesser problems

Wet rot (4 advanced stage)

You are almost certain to find this problem appearing somewhere on your property. Wet rot is caused by continuous saturation of wood such as where fence posts are buried in the soil. Often the first sign, on painted wood, is blisters under the paint surface. The paint can be peeled off revealing damp wood underneath and the wood feels spongy when pressed. On windows in particular this can be caused by the putty shrinking away from the glass and allowing rain to seep into the frame. Badly affected timber can be cut out and replaced, but wood that is damp but sound should have

the paint burnt off and then be left to dry in the summer sun, after which it can be painted with the proper primer and undercoat (see page 14).

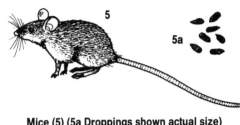

Mice (5) (5a Droppings shown actual size)

House mice are more of a nuisance than a danger but they can spoil food and nibble through electric cables. The household cat can earn its keep by keeping mice down but once again good household hygiene will deter them. Never leave uneaten food out in the house; store perishables in the fridge and dry foods in secure cupboards and don't leave plates dirty overnight.

Cockroach (6)

Cockroaches are flat shiny creatures that scuttle noisily at night in warm kitchens when the light is suddenly turned on. They can contaminate large amounts of food and once again good hygiene will defeat them. Don't leave any scraps of food whatsoever lying about at night.

Wasp (7) (7a Wasp nest showing inner comb and outer shell)

Although most people are terrified of wasps—and bees—the wasp is quite beneficial to the gardener as it carries off large numbers of insects back to its nest colony. It is only in late summer that the wasp becomes a nuisance, when the brood raising is complete and it turns its attentions to sweet sticky things. However if wasps build a nest in your house or outbuildings it can become a hazard due to the large numbers involved and it is best to call in a specialist with the proper equipment to destroy it.

Ant (8)

Ants only become a nuisance when armies of them march into your kitchen to carry off sugar grains or such like. Stop up any holes and put down ant killer if they bother you.

Animal flea (9)

Tiny bloodsucking insects: the ones you are most likely to come into contact with are cat fleas and dog fleas. They cannot live on humans but they can bite you. Treat pets with a flea powder and change their bedding regularly.

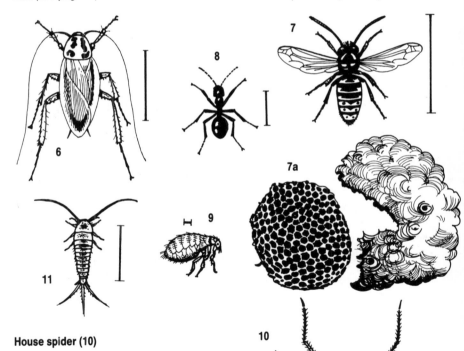

House spider (10)

Although some people dislike spiders they are definitely a friend as they trap large numbers of flies in their webs. If you find one in the bath trap it in a glass covered with paper and place it outside to continue its good work. They cannot harm you.

Silverfish (11)

These are the little torpedo-shaped creatures that move rapidly across walls and floors when you turn the light on in the bathroom at night. They feed on wallpaper pastes and detritus and are completely harmless.

Note. The line alongside the insect drawings denotes actual size.

83

Insulation

Two of the easiest and most cost-effective savings you can make to your home are by ensuring that it is firstly, draught-proofed and secondly, properly insulated. Because we don't suffer the extremes of temperature of continental Europe we tend to take a much more ambivalent attitude to insulation than the rest of northern Europe. Consequently our homes are among the least thermally efficient. Government regulations now stipulate that all new buildings conform to a minimum standard with regard to insulation, but that leaves the rest of us to do what we can.

Stopping heat losses

The first priority in insulation terms is the stopping of draughts as, particularly on a windy day, heat can be sucked out of the house almost as quickly as it is produced. One thing to consider though is that too efficient draught–proofing can cause condensation, as the circulation of air in rooms is drastically reduced. Open fires won't burn properly and if you have open-flued boilers there may be a dangerous build-up of fumes. Controlled ventilation is the ideal, through windows and vents.

Local authorities will give grants towards the cost of insulating a home but you must contact them before the work is done—not after. Water and central heating pipes, particularly those in out-of-the-way places like under floors and in lofts, must be properly insulated, not only against heat losses but also to prevent freezing in very cold weather. Do not, under any circumstances, seal air bricks under floors: you may encourage dry rot.

Roofs 25%

Walls 35%

Windows 15%

Doors 10%

Floors 15%

Under-door weather and draught proofing

There are several different designs to solve the difficult problem of sealing draughts under exterior doors. Most consist of an aluminium extrusion with neoprene or brush inserts. Some are designed to replace the wooden door seal. Most will require careful fitting to be effective and you may have to plane the door bottom to ensure a good fit.

A. Threshold and doorseal kit. A neoprene insert butts against the door to complete the seal under an extruded aluminium weather bar.
B. Brush excluder. A nylon brush strip seals any irregularities betwen the floor and the existing sill.
C. Bottom sealing excluder. A neoprene seal fits into an aluminium moulding, screwed in position under the door.

Exterior

A

Weather bar

Neoprene insert

B

Nylon brush

Exterior

Existing sill

C

Neoprene insert

D. Draught seals for fitting around doors and windows. A soft, moulded rubber strip which is cut to length and inserted into loose frames for the duration of winter. Easily removed in summer and re-useable.
E. PVC foam self-adhesive strip. The cheapest and simplest form of draught stripping. Simply peel off the backing strip and stick in the door or window rebates. Various thicknesses are available for different-sized gaps.
F. Nylon brush pile strip. Self-adhesive: cut to length and stick in rebates. Does not compress to the same extent as PVC foam.
G. V-strip (metal or plastic). This is pinned into the rebate and is compressed by the door to complete the seal.

D E F G

Insulation

Loft insulation

Laying loft insulation is not a difficult job, but it can be messy and unpleasant if you don't take precautions. Glass-fibre insulation can irritate the skin—so wear rubber gloves. You are also likely to disturb a certain amount of dust so it's worth wearing a simple face mask with replaceable filters and a boiler suit to keep your clothes clean. Rig up some temporary lighting so that you can see clearly what you are doing. The minimum recommended thickness of loft insulation is 100 mm (4 in) and you will probably find that this comes level with the joists when laid. Don't forget to insulate the trapdoor.

Pipe insulation

This consists mainly of two types. The first, preformed flexible foam tubes sized for 15 mm and 22 mm pipes, are taped into place and mitred at pipe junctions to make a very neat and permanent job. They are usually sold in packs containing 1 m (39 in) lengths. The second is a wrap-around lagging made either from glass-fibre, similar to loft insulation, or felt. This is wrapped around the pipe, overlapping as you go, and secured by tape or string.

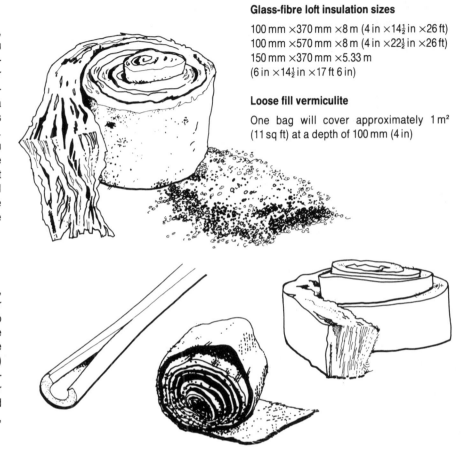

Glass-fibre loft insulation sizes

100 mm ×370 mm ×8 m (4 in ×14½ in ×26 ft)
100 mm ×570 mm ×8 m (4 in ×22½ in ×26 ft)
150 mm ×370 mm ×5.33 m
(6 in ×14½ in ×17 ft 6 in)

Loose fill vermiculite

One bag will cover approximately 1 m² (11 sq ft) at a depth of 100 mm (4 in)

Hot water cylinder jacket

These are clipped around the cylinder, secured with plastic straps, and tied at the top. If buying a new cylinder get one with a polystyrene coating.

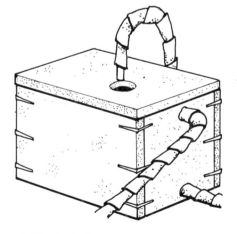

Cold water tank

Expanded polystyrene slabs are available for insulating the cold water tank. These can be secured by special clips or taped into place. If the tank is round, then wrap it with glass-fibre loft insulation, tied on with string. Don't forget the lid.

Other insulation

Double-glazing is, of course, a well-known but expensive way of reducing heat loss and is usually carried out by contractors. As walls are responsible for such a large proportion of heat losses everything possible should be done to reduce this. Cavity walls can be injected with foam by specialist contractors, but solid walls present an almost impossible problem. Interior insulation by wallboards—on battens over glass-fibre blanket—is possible, but it's a big job. It also reduces room sizes and skirting boards, sockets and wall lights must be moved. Exterior wall insulation poses similar problems with pipes and window sills and is only worth considering if you are having your property re-rendered.

Security

Improving living standards over recent years has meant a greater proportion of high value—and portable—equipment can be found in even modest homes and this had lead to an ever increasing risk of burglaries. Fortunately there are now some very good locks and security devices available for DIY fitting. Take care before buying to ensure that any door or window locks will fit your frames.

Doors

Older properties are often fitted with only a rim latch (the sort of lock that allows you to slam the door but without a handle on the outside) on the front door and a two-lever mortise lock on the back door. These should be replaced by deadlocks (locks which can be locked by a key from both sides and cannot be opened without that key).

With front doors the old rim latch can either be left in place with a mortise deadlock fitted below it, or a high-security deadlocking rim latch can be fitted in place of it.

An explanation of rim latches and mortise locks

A rim latch is fitted to the inner surface of the door with a large hole drilled through the door to accept the cylinder. A mortise lock is fitted into the stile (side frame) of the door with keyholes only on the outside and inside of the door.

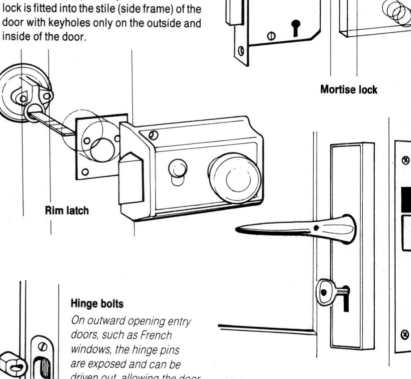

Mortise lock

Rim latch

Modern high-security deadlocking rim latch
Available with slam facility.

Security chain

Limits the opening of a door, giving you a chance to identify callers. Get a strong one and make sure it's secured with good long screws.

Hinge bolts

On outward opening entry doors, such as French windows, the hinge pins are exposed and can be driven out, allowing the door to be levered open from the hinge side. With two of these fitted near the hinges the door remains secure.

High security mortise deadlock

Get a lock with at least a five-lever mechanism—two-lever locks are not secure enough for external doors. Fitting a mortise lock requires expert woodworking skills. If you are not competent have it professionally fitted.

Door viewer

Simply fitted at eye-level by drilling a single hole in solid doors, it allows a wide angle view of the outside so that you can check the identity of callers.

Door limiter

*A strong metal sliding catch which can be used in place of a door chain.
The door must be closed before the stay can be flipped over to release the door.*

Security

Windows

Windows are the favourite point of entry and if casements (side-hinged windows) and sashes (vertical sliding windows) are locked, the thief must break a pane of glass—something he will only do as a last resort because of the noise. Make sure that your frames are sound. Rotten windows are easily levered open.

By far the majority of window locks are designed for timber windows, but some of the locks shown here are made for metal windows in which case they are secured by self-tapping screws.

Aluminium replacement windows are difficult to secure because of the softness of the material. So if you are having new windows installed make sure they come with good quality locking systems.

Louvre windows are particularly difficult to secure because the panes can be easily levered out. Consider gluing them into their frames with epoxy resin (see page 81).

Cockspur handle locks

There are various methods of locking the cockspur handle (the small lever on the side of casement windows) including a key-operated replacement handle. This one has a pivoting cover, which flips back when unlocked to release the handle.

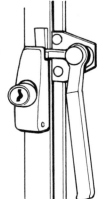

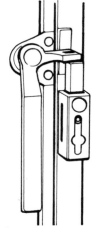

Mortise door and window bolts

Suitable for timber doors and windows, these neat and unobtrusive locks are fitted into the frame, and a racked bolt is wound out with a key.

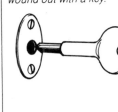

Sliding cockspur lock

This version is for metal windows. The sliding bar locates under the cockspur and is locked in position.

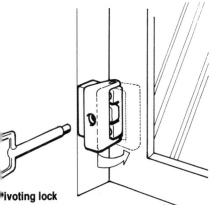

Pivoting lock

The pivoting catch is swung over and locked against the bracket with a special key. Versions available for metal and timber casements.

Wedge lock

A very neat lock for metal casement windows. Simple to fit and hidden from view, it fits in the window channel and is operated by a simple key through a small hole on the inside.

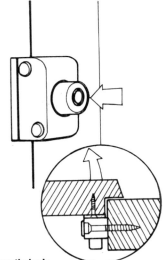

Automatic lock

Closing the window locks the device automatically. It can be opened using a special slotted key. It is supplied with a wedged plate for fitting to a tapered frame.

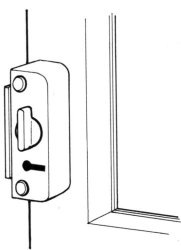

Key-operated casement lock

The window can be secured by turning the catch. A key is used to unlock the window.

Fire safety

Bear in mind when fitting security bolts to doors and windows that in case of fire you do need to get your family out very quickly—and searching for keys in a panic is not recommended. Therefore always keep keys in the same place and make sure every member of the family knows where this is. Don't leave keys in locks as this defeats the whole object of security.

Security 2

Some of the locks described for casement windows can be used on sliding sashes, but there are some specially designed ones for sash windows.

A. Dual screws. Neat and unobtrusive in use and simple to fit. A key-operated bolt screws through a brass bush in the inner frame and into a second bush in the outer frame. Used in pairs.

B. Brighton fastener. A simple hand operated screw-down catch that is used in place of the standard fitch fastener.

C. Locking fitch. This replaces the usual cam fitch, but is key-lockable.

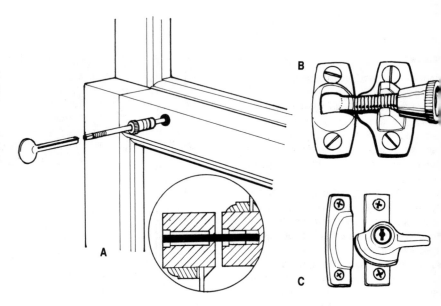

Fanlights

Fanlights (the horizontally-hinged windows above doors) are another favourite point of entry, mainly because they are often left open for ventilation during hot weather and even when closed are only secured by the fanlight stay. Some of the casement locks can be used on fanlights, but the favourite design seems to be locking the stay.

There are two types of stay; those with holes and those without and two different designs of lock to suit. Some types can lock the window in a partially open position.

D and **E** are for stays with holes and **F** is for stays without holes.

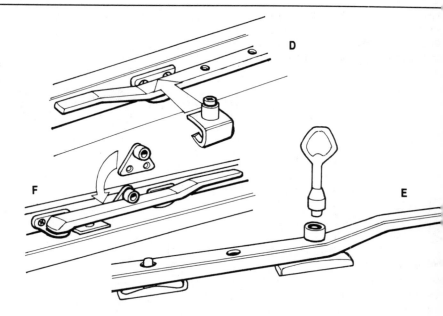

Patio doors

One of the problems associated with patio doors is that they can be levered up out of their track. So when fitting locks, which is a relatively easy task, take this into consideration and position the locks where they will restrict this.

The best type of lock shoots a bolt into the fixed frame from the sliding frame and is secured with self-tapping screws. Take careful measurements of your own doors before buying any lock, to make sure that it will fit your particular situation.

G and **H** show two types of neat and unobtrusive patio door locks.

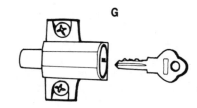

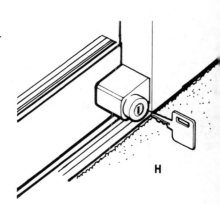

Security 2

Burglar alarms

There are many burglar alarm systems now available, ranging from simple DIY kits to sophisticated electronic systems installed by specialist security firms. What you choose must be determined by your needs and lifestyle. The effectiveness of any alarm system is degraded if it's set off regularly by naturaly causes—like high winds and lightning—and neighbours can get annoyed by a less than perfect system. Therefore go for the best you can afford and stick to well-known names. Your local Crime Prevention Officer will advise you which are the best types.

Some alarm systems incorporate a panic button which will sound the alarm, and these can be situated near the door or bed. These can be comforting to the elderly and those living alone.

Security lighting

Although daytime break-ins are not uncommon, most intruders prefer the cover of darkness and good outside lighting will certainly reduce the risk of night-time burglaries. Fortunately there are now some excellent and highly sophisticated security lighting systems on the market. Most are not difficult to fit, but some knowledge of electric wiring is necessary.

Front and back entrance doors should always be well lit, not only from the security point of view but for reasons of safety as well.

Timers and photo–electric cells can be wired into exterior and interior lights to switch them on and off while you're away. A newer introduction is the Passive Infra-red Sensor. Exterior light fittings incorporating one of these can detect body heat and illuminate the area with bright light immediately—a powerful deterrent to a would-be thief.

Follow the fitting instructions carefully regarding siting, or you could annoy neighbours and legitimate passers-by. Security lights with sensors are available in both modern and antique designs to suit the decor of your home.

Security marking

Although marking your property is unlikely to stop it being stolen, you are at least much more likely to get it back. The police recover an enormous amount of stolen property and always have difficulty tracing the proper owners as it often ends up in another part of the country.

The accepted marking is your postcode followed by the number of your house—or the first three letters of your house name if it doesn't have a number. That is all that is required.

There are basically two methods of marking property. The first is engraving it with a diamond-tipped pen and a stencil and the second using a UV marker. Marks made with a UV marker are invisible in ordinary circumstances but can be read easily under a special Ultra-violet light.

Note. Before engraving antique gold or silver items get advice from your local Crime Prevention Officer. You should think carefully before marking these as it may affect their re-sale value.

Fire protection

FIRE

Smoke detectors

The first defence against fire in the home is the installation of one or more smoke alarms. They are cheap, easy to fit and will detect smoke far quicker than you will. There are many models now available. Get one with a built-in escape light and a test button for regular battery checking. Follow the manufacturer's instructions when fitting—particularly regarding positioning as there are optimum areas for smoke detection throughout the house.

Fire extinguishers

A fitted fire extinguisher is a good idea in the kitchen and workshop or garage. Your choice should be made from either vaporizing liquid (Halon) or dry powder types, as these can both be used on electrical and fat fires as well as ordinary combustible materials.

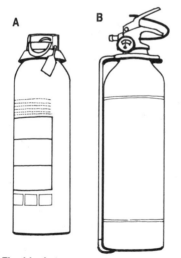
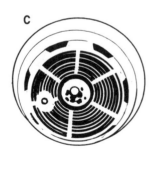
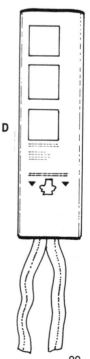

A. Halon fire extinguisher
B. Dry powder extinguisher
C. Smoke alarm
D. Fire blanket

Fire blanket

A good alternative to the fire extinguisher in the kitchen is the fire blanket. A quick pull on the hanging tapes releases the glass-fibre blanket which can be thrown over a chip-pan fire, for example, starving it of oxygen and keeping mess to a minimum. It can also be re-used.

89

Ladders

Ladders
Modern aluminium ladders are light, strong and easy to handle. They are also very durable.

75°

For maximum stability a ladder should lean at approximately 75° or a quarter of the extended height out from the wall.

All the equipment shown is available for hire. Check the Yellow Pages for local stockists and get their lists so as to compare availability and prices.

A deposit will be required and a same day delivery service is usually available.

Ladder stay
This clamps securely to the top rungs of a ladder and holds it away from the wall, to give clearance when working on gutters and eaves. Rubber grips give added security.

Stepladder
Indispensable inside and out. Lightweight aluminium ones are best. Top step/platform heights run from 0.80 m (2 ft 8 in) high upwards.

Combination stepladder
Various configurations are available which convert from being a standard stepladder to a short ladder and also to a stair ladder for use on different levels.

Ladder sizes – Two section
Ladders are available for hire but if you do much outside maintenance it's better to buy.
2.6 m extends to 4.30 m
(8 ft 6 in extends to 14 ft 10 in)
3.20 m extends to 5.60 m
(10 ft 5 in extends to 18 ft 6 in)
3.4 m extends to 6.2 m
(11 ft 4 in extends to 20 ft 3 in)
4 m extends to 7.3 m
(13 ft extends 23 ft 11 in)
4.5 m extends to 8.4 m
(14 ft 11 in extends to 27 ft 6 in)
The 4 m size is about the most useful for the average two-storey house. For most people larger sizes are too unwieldy to use alone.

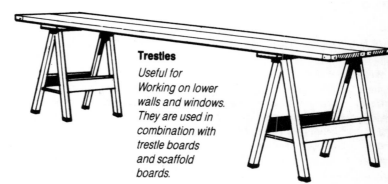

Trestles
Useful for Working on lower walls and windows. They are used in combination with trestle boards and scaffold boards.

Access equipment

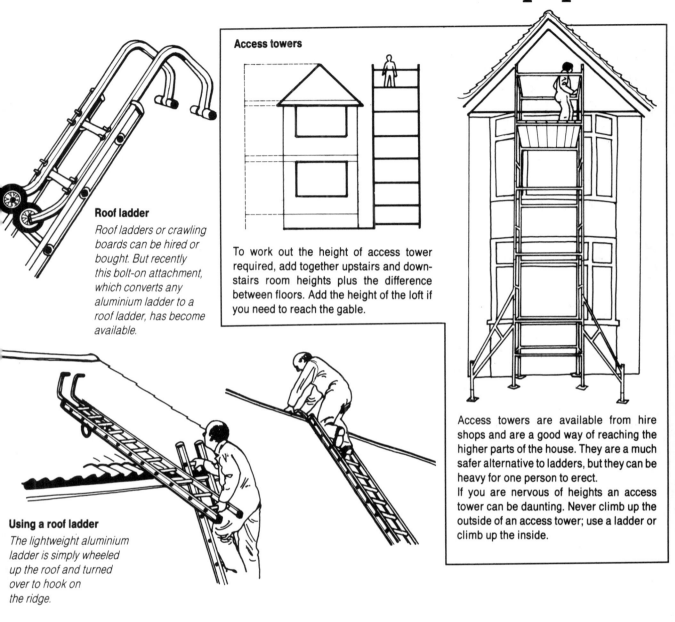

Roof ladder

Roof ladders or crawling boards can be hired or bought. But recently this bolt-on attachment, which converts any aluminium ladder to a roof ladder, has become available.

Access towers

To work out the height of access tower required, add together upstairs and downstairs room heights plus the difference between floors. Add the height of the loft if you need to reach the gable.

Using a roof ladder

The lightweight aluminium ladder is simply wheeled up the roof and turned over to hook on the ridge.

Access towers are available from hire shops and are a good way of reaching the higher parts of the house. They are a much safer alternative to ladders, but they can be heavy for one person to erect.

If you are nervous of heights an access tower can be daunting. Never climb up the outside of an access tower; use a ladder or climb up the inside.

What size skip?

For removal of large amounts of building or garden rubbish, skip hire is the well-tried method. Conditions vary but generally a flat rate is charged for the size of skip and there is no time limit. Three main sizes are of interest to the householder – Maxi, Midi and Mini.

The approximate capacities are as follows:

Maxi   4.6 m³ (6 cubic yards)
Midi   3.0 m³ (4 cubic yards)
Mini   1.5 m³ (2 cubic yards)

A garden wheelbarrow will hold approximately 0.75 m³ (2¾ cubic feet) and a builder's barrow 0.85 m³ (3 cubic feet).

Large skips may have a drop front for easier loading. Local Authorities may require a permit and lighting for skips left on the public highway. Check first.

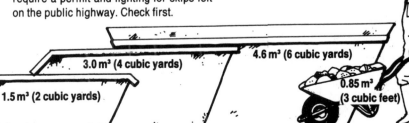

3.0 m³ (4 cubic yards)
4.6 m³ (6 cubic yards)
1.5 m³ (2 cubic yards)
0.85 m³ (3 cubic feet)

Tiles

Re-roofing a house is definitely not a DIY job, but from time to time it may be necessary to replace a broken tile or slate and perhaps do other small repair jobs. If you don't mind working at heights and are willing to hire the necessary access equipment, tile and slate replacement is relatively easy. Pitched roofs are clad commonly with either clay tiles, concrete tiles or slate. Natural roofing materials tend to reflect the area of the country in which the building is situated but man-made materials can be found everywhere.

Remove the old tile or slate and take it to a specialist roofing contractor to match the replacement. They usually have a retail counter for this purpose. Older clay tiles and natural slates can sometimes be found at building reclamation specialists. Look in Yellow Pages.

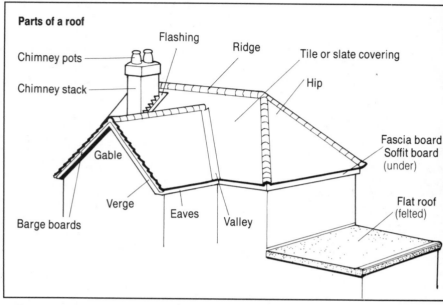

Parts of a roof

Chimney pots — Flashing — Ridge — Tile or slate covering

Chimney stack — Hip

Gable — Fascia board / Soffit board (under)

Verge — Eaves — Valley

Barge boards — Flat roof (felted)

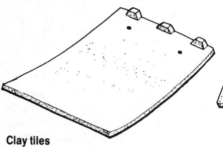

Clay tiles

Underside of a clay tile showing curvature—to repel capillary action of rain-water—and the nibs which lock over the timber battens to hold the tile in place.

Tile shapes

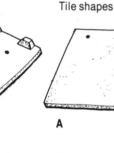
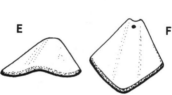

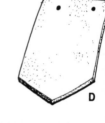

A   B   C   D

E   F   G   H

I   J

Tip

To remove a damaged tile, slide wedges under the tiles above it, so the nibs can be raised clear of the batten and the tile slid out. Use a slate ripper if it's nailed.

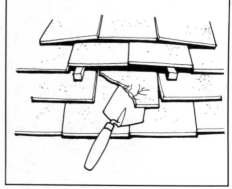

Tile shapes

A. Tile and a half. Clay tiles are laid in staggered courses, like bricks, and a 'tile and a half' is used at the roof verge to stagger the row.

B. Plain tile. Ordinary tile.

C. Club. D. Arrowhead. Used for vertical tile hanging.

E. Bonnet hip tile. Tile used on the ridge of a hipped roof.

F. Hip tile. Another version of the above.

G. Angle ridge H. Ridge tile. Two types of ridge tile.

I. Valley tile. Used at the junction of two pitched roofs.

J. Interlocking concrete tiles. Modern interlocking tiles are not staggered. Waterproofing is achieved by the moulded edge of a tile lying over its neighbour.

Slates

Tile and slate sizes and coverage

Tiles in common use are available in the following sizes:

Plain tiles; 265×165 mm ($10\frac{1}{2} \times 6\frac{1}{2}$ in). Tiles per square metre—60. Shorter tiles for eaves courses are 190×165 mm ($7\frac{1}{2} \times 6\frac{1}{2}$ in) and 'tile and a half' tiles are 265×250 mm ($10\frac{1}{2} \times 10$ in).

Half-round ridge tiles are available in 300 and 455 mm (12 and 18 in) lengths and diameters of 80 mm (3 in), 100 mm (4 in), 150 mm (6 in), 200 mm (8 in), 230 mm (9 in) and 255 mm (10 in).

Interlocking concrete tiles are larger and heavier and are available in the following sizes:

430×380 mm (17×15 in). Tiles per square metre—8.2. 420×330 mm ($16\frac{1}{2} \times 13$ in). Tiles per square metre—9.7. 380×230 mm (15×9 in). Tiles per square metre—16.5.

There are about nine sizes available in slates. They range from 610×305 mm (24×12 in) down to 355×180 mm (14×7 in) and in three weights of: Standard—5.1 mm (approx. $\frac{1}{5}$ in), Heavy—6.3 mm (approx. $\frac{1}{4}$ in) and Extra Heavy—8.5 mm (approx. $\frac{1}{3}$ in). Older sizes are even more varied.

Slates

Slates are split from natural stone and unlike plain tiles are perfectly flat. The usual reason for slates slipping is corroded nails. You cannot wedge up slates like tiles as they will crack. Therefore use a slate ripper to remove old nails and then remove the broken slate. Use a strip of lead or zinc nailed between the two underlying slates, slide the new slate in position, align the bottom and bend the zinc or lead strip up and over to secure.

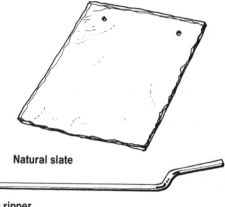

Natural slate

Slate ripper

Using a slate ripper

A slate ripper is a special tool designed to get at the inaccessible nails holding slates and tiles in place. They can be bought but it's probably better to hire one.
Slide it under the slate to locate the sharpened hook behind the nail and pull sharply to break the nail.

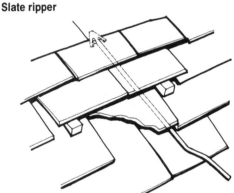

Roof flashings

Roof flashings are used for waterproofing where pitched roofs adjoin vertical brickwork as, for example, around a chimney stack. Lead was, and often still is, the preferred material for this situation, being soft and malleable and resistant to corrosion and air pollution. Zinc and soft aluminium are also used as is bituminized felt—the latter particularly on flat roofs.

Replacing flashings is not a DIY job as certain skills are needed, however repairs to corroded and leaky flashings can be made and special materials and kits have been developed for just such a purpose. These materials have been manufactured and tested to stick well to existing flashings like lead and zinc and should always be used in preference to something you may have left over from some other job.

Flashing tape sizes
Sizes commonly available to the DIY market are as follows:
Self-adhesive
75 mm $\times 2.5$ m (3 in $\times 8$ ft)
100 mm $\times 2.5$ m (4 in $\times 8$ ft)
150 mm $\times 2.5$ m (6 in $\times 8$ ft)
225 mm $\times 2.5$ mm (9 in $\times 8$ ft)
All the above are available in 4 m (13 ft) rolls also.

Non-hardening waterproof tapes for use over roofing glazing bars
50 mm $\times 4$ m (2 in $\times 13$ ft)

Clear weatherproofing tape for sealing overlaps in transluscent roofing and repairs to roof glass
38 mm $\times 6$ m ($1\frac{1}{2}$ in $\times 20$ ft)
75 mm $\times 6$ m (3 in $\times 20$ ft)

Roof repair tapes for sealing asphalt and felt roofs
100 mm $\times 2.5$ m (4 in $\times 8$ ft)
150 mm $\times 2.5$ m (6 in $\times 8$ ft)

Corrugated roofing

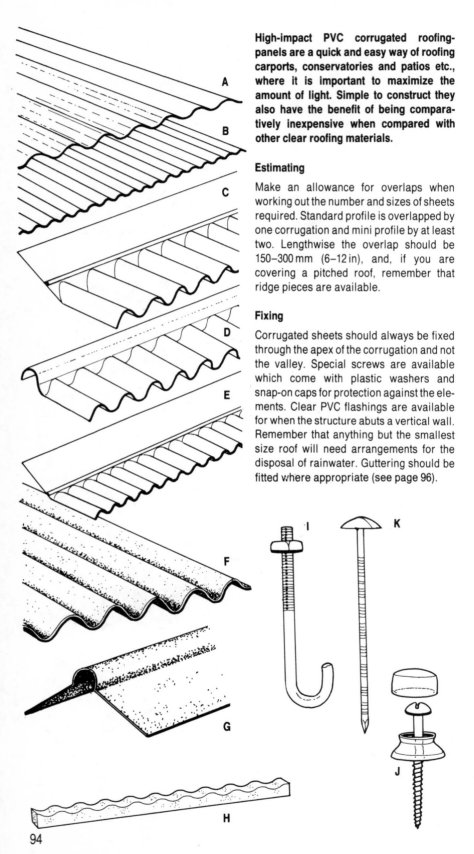

High-impact PVC corrugated roofing-panels are a quick and easy way of roofing carports, conservatories and patios etc., where it is important to maximize the amount of light. Simple to construct they also have the benefit of being comparatively inexpensive when compared with other clear roofing materials.

Estimating

Make an allowance for overlaps when working out the number and sizes of sheets required. Standard profile is overlapped by one corrugation and mini profile by at least two. Lengthwise the overlap should be 150–300 mm (6–12 in), and, if you are covering a pitched roof, remember that ridge pieces are available.

Fixing

Corrugated sheets should always be fixed through the apex of the corrugation and not the valley. Special screws are available which come with plastic washers and snap-on caps for protection against the elements. Clear PVC flashings are available for when the structure abuts a vertical wall. Remember that anything but the smallest size roof will need arrangements for the disposal of rainwater. Guttering should be fitted where appropriate (see page 96).

Bituminized corrugated roofing

Bituminized corrugated roofing sheets are a new development and are made from organic and inorganic fibres saturated with bitumen under intense pressure and heat to form strong rigid sheets.

They are light in weight, asbestos free, impact resistant, not affected by chemicals, will not rot, are resistant to frost and have a guaranteed life of 15 years. They can be cut easily with a saw and are fixed by nailing directly through the panels with PVC-headed nails, which form a watertight seal. They are available in matt black, brown and a dull green which has a weathered look and does not look out of place in the garden. Added to this they are relatively inexpensive.

Sizes

PVC clear corrugated sheets

Standard profile 75 mm (3 in)
760 mm (30 in) wide × 1.8 m (6ft), 2.4 m (8 ft) and 3 m (10 ft)
Mini profile 32 mm (1¼ in)
760 m (30 in) wide × 1.8 m (6 ft), 2.4 m (8 ft) and 3 m (10 ft).

Bituminized corrugated roofing sheets

900 mm (35 in) × 2 m (78 in).

A. Standard profile clear PVC corrugated roofing 75 mm (3 in)
B. Mini profile clear PVC corrugated roofing 32 mm (1¼ in)
C. Matching flashing piece for standard profile
D. Matching ridge piece for standard profile
E. Matching flashing piece for mini profile
F. Bituminized corrugated roofing
G. Matching ridge piece for bituminized corrugated sheeting
H. Plastic foam eaves filler strip for standard profile
I. U-bolt for fixing roofing to angle iron supports
J. Screw with washer and cap for fixing PVC corrugated roofing
K. PVC-headed nail for fixing bituminized corrugated roofing.

Flat roofs

Polycarbonate sheet

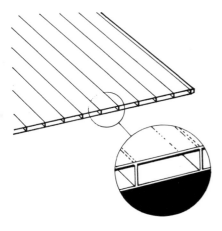

Another type of translucent roofing which can be used in conservatories as an alternative to glass is polycarbonate sheeting. It was originally developed to combat vandalism and is virtually unbreakable. Twinwall and triplewall types also have excellent insulation properties, so, although it cannot equal the clarity of glass, it outperforms the latter in many ways.

When cutting polycarbonate care must be taken to avoid getting swarf and moisture in the exposed channels. Special glazing systems exist for the fitting of panels which allow for the thermal expansion of the sheets.

Check out mail order supply specialists for more detailed information.

Polycarbonate sheeting can also be used for greenhouses and cold frames where its good insulation and strength can be appreciated.

Sizes

Sizes vary between different suppliers, but some of the available sizes are as follows:
Twinwall
700 mm ×3 m ×10 mm (28 in ×10 ft ×$\frac{3}{8}$ in),
925 mm ×3 m ×10 mm (3 ft ×10 ft ×$\frac{3}{8}$ in),
1.05 m ×4 m ×10 mm (41 in ×13 ft ×$\frac{3}{8}$ in),
970 mm ×4 m ×10 mm (38 in ×13 ft ×$\frac{3}{8}$ in).
Triplewall
1.05 m ×3 m ×16 mm (41 in ×10 ft ×$\frac{5}{8}$ in),
1.05 m ×4 m ×16 mm (41 in ×13 ft ×$\frac{5}{8}$ in).

Roofing felts

Simple felt roofs

Roofing sheds and outhouses is a very simple task and the roll of felt will usually come with printed instructions on how to proceed and for which type of building it is suitable.

Roofing felts are classified in five classes under BS747. However, as far as the DIYer is concerned, only Class 1 is likely to be of interest and easily available. The other classes are for use by the trade each having its own purpose and attributes.

Sizes

The standard size roll of felt is 1 m × 10 m (39 in × 33 ft) and the following weights are available: 14 kg, 18 kg, 25 kg and 38 kg. They come in black or an attractive dull green—which goes well in the garden—and have either a sand or a mineral finish.

Large-headed clout nails (see page 73) are used for fixing and you will need felt adhesive as well. Follow the manufacturer's instructions for fixing.

The ideal time for roofing sheds etc, is a hot summer day. Cut the lengths, slightly oversize, and lay them out in the sun. They will expand to their maximum and when laid will shrink as the temperature falls to give a flat finish.

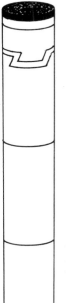

Flat roofs

Flat roofs are commonly used for house extensions. They consist of a 19 mm ($\frac{3}{4}$ in) chipboard decking over joists which is covered with three layers of bituminized felt and often finished with granite chippings to reflect the sun's heat. The whole is bonded together by hot bitumen. Specialist contractors should be used as this is obviously not a job for the amateur.

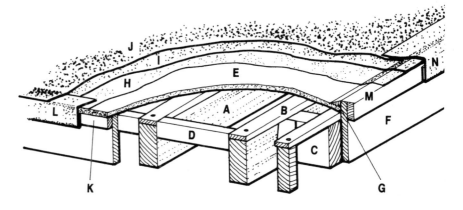

A. Joists
B. Furring pieces
C. Return joists
D. Nogging
E. Decking
F. Fascia
G. Angle fillet

H. 1st felt layer
I. 2nd felt layer
J. Capsheet with granite chippings
K. Eaves drip batten
L. Felt eaves drip
M. Verge drip batten
N. Felt verge drip

Guttering

There is sometimes confusion among householders about rain-water disposal systems and household waste-water disposal systems. The two are completely separate. If you study the drawing on page 67 you will see how the pipework in your own property relates to household waste-water disposal. This is connected to the main sewer or a septic tank.

Guttering is for the collection and disposal of rain-water and is not usually connected to the sewer, although in some cases there may be a storm drain constructed for rain-water disposal. Nowadays rain-water is directed to a soakaway in the soil somewhere.

It's very important to keep guttering in good order and not allow leaks to go unattended. If you ignore faults it can lead, over a period of time, to dampness in walls and deterioration of brickwork and plaster, as well as to the growth of unsightly algae on exterior surfaces.

When inspecting or working on guttering use a ladder stay (see page 90) to keep the ladder away from the wall—never lean a ladder against guttering—it's just not safe. There are various waterproofing and repair materials available for small repair jobs, so it's not difficult to keep your guttering watertight. Of course, if modern guttering is damaged it's quite a simple matter to replace the damaged section, but if you live in an older property with attractive cast-iron guttering it may be worth keeping it for as long as possible. There are non-hardening mastics which can be pressed into the leaky joints, and self-adhesive flashing tape which can be wrapped around cracked downpipes. Alternatively you could use epoxy resin or glass-fibre car repair filler—which can be filed to shape after hardening and painted—to make an almost invisible repair. Although a big job, it is not difficult to replace old guttering with new uPVC (unplasticized polyvinyl chloride) guttering. The biggest problem is likely to be the removal of the old guttering, particularly if this is cast-iron. The screws and bolts holding it all together are likely to be rusted and will need to be sawn through.

Cast-iron is quite heavy and you should not try to remove this on your own. You need two people up two separate ladders to lower it safely to the ground. By comparison uPVC guttering is featherweight and easily handled by one person.

Of course you are likely to find after you've taken the guttering down that the exposed fascia boards need repainting, so the job may turn out longer than anticipated.

Installation

Modern uPVC guttering is very simple to install and most types work on a system of interlocking clips with neoprene inserts to seal the joints. However, like plastic plumbing mentioned elsewhere, systems from different manufacturers are not usually compatible. Once again the best bet is to visit your local DIY store or builders' merchants to see which type predominates and select your system from this. Instruction leaflets are often supplied by manufacturers and these contain installation instructions as well as an illustrated list of the parts available.

Guttering types

The commonest material for modern guttering is uPVC and this may be available in black, white, grey and brown and in half-round or square section.

Cast-iron guttering is still made for renovating period properties, but may take some searching out. Enquire at good builders' merchants. It will, of course, be expensive. Cast-aluminium is a cheaper alternative that requires very little maintenance.

Sheet aluminium is manufactured on-site by specialist contractors and has the advantage of long gutter runs without joins. Asbestos-cement guttering is unusual nowadays due to health risks and if you are removing such a system you should contact your local environmental health officer for advice on safe disposal.

Guttering shapes and sizes

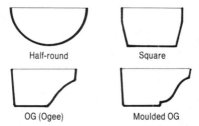

Half-round   Square

OG (Ogee)   Moulded OG

Three basic shapes are usually found in guttering; half-round, OG (Ogee) and square section. There is sometimes a variation on the OG shape, known as moulded OG.

Sizes

Guttering is usually described by its width across and in square section by its depth also.

uPVC

Half-round: 75 mm (3 in), 100 mm (4 in), 112 mm (4½ in) and 150 mm (6 in).
Square: 100 × 75 mm (4 × 3 in) and 112 × 75 mm (4½ × 3 in).

Cast-aluminium

Half-round and OG: 112 mm (4½ in).

Cast-iron

Half-round and OG: 100 mm (4 in), 112 mm (4½ in) and 125 m (5 in).

The smallest size, 75 mm guttering, is used for sheds and garages and the larger sizes for houses. Generally replace with a similar size to what is already there.

Tip

Fit a balloon grating into the top of the downpipe to stop it becoming blocked with leaves or debris.

Guttering

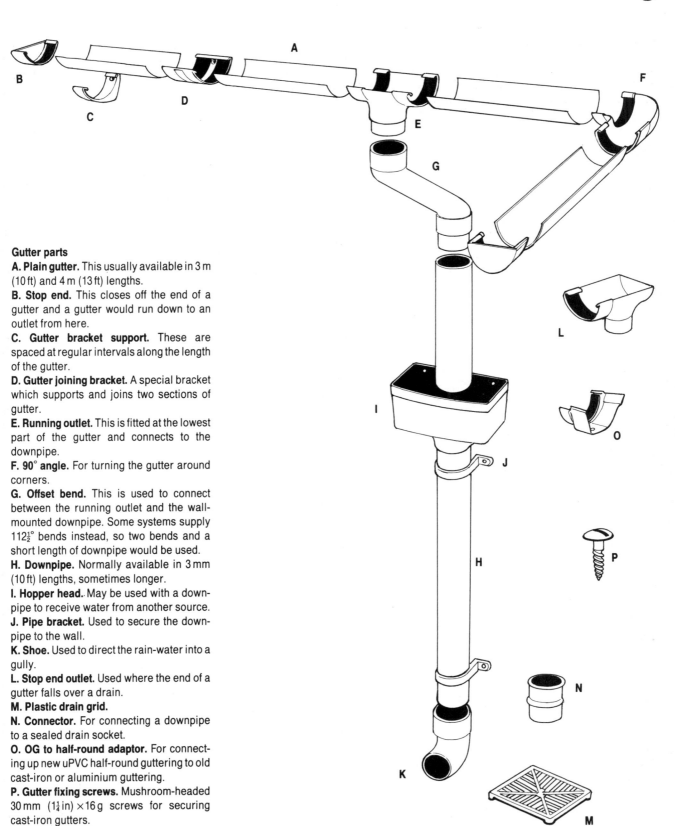

Gutter parts

A. Plain gutter. This usually available in 3 m (10 ft) and 4 m (13 ft) lengths.

B. Stop end. This closes off the end of a gutter and a gutter would run down to an outlet from here.

C. Gutter bracket support. These are spaced at regular intervals along the length of the gutter.

D. Gutter joining bracket. A special bracket which supports and joins two sections of gutter.

E. Running outlet. This is fitted at the lowest part of the gutter and connects to the downpipe.

F. 90° angle. For turning the gutter around corners.

G. Offset bend. This is used to connect between the running outlet and the wall-mounted downpipe. Some systems supply $112\frac{1}{2}°$ bends instead, so two bends and a short length of downpipe would be used.

H. Downpipe. Normally available in 3 mm (10 ft) lengths, sometimes longer.

I. Hopper head. May be used with a downpipe to receive water from another source.

J. Pipe bracket. Used to secure the downpipe to the wall.

K. Shoe. Used to direct the rain-water into a gully.

L. Stop end outlet. Used where the end of a gutter falls over a drain.

M. Plastic drain grid.

N. Connector. For connecting a downpipe to a sealed drain socket.

O. OG to half-round adaptor. For connecting up new uPVC half-round guttering to old cast-iron or aluminium guttering.

P. Gutter fixing screws. Mushroom-headed 30 mm ($1\frac{1}{4}$ in) ×16 g screws for securing cast-iron gutters.

Concrete

Most householders can confidently do their own concreting. Unless the job is large it's fairly easy and quite satisfying but it's important to use the correct materials in the correct proportions to achieve good results. The strength of concrete depends on the mixing, which should be very thorough. Avoid doing concrete work when there is a risk of frost, and don't skimp on sub-bases for economic reasons. When concrete cracks, it's usually through lack of support.

Estimating quantities

From the area to be covered, on the left, read across to the intended thickness. From where these lines cross read down to give the total volume of concrete required.

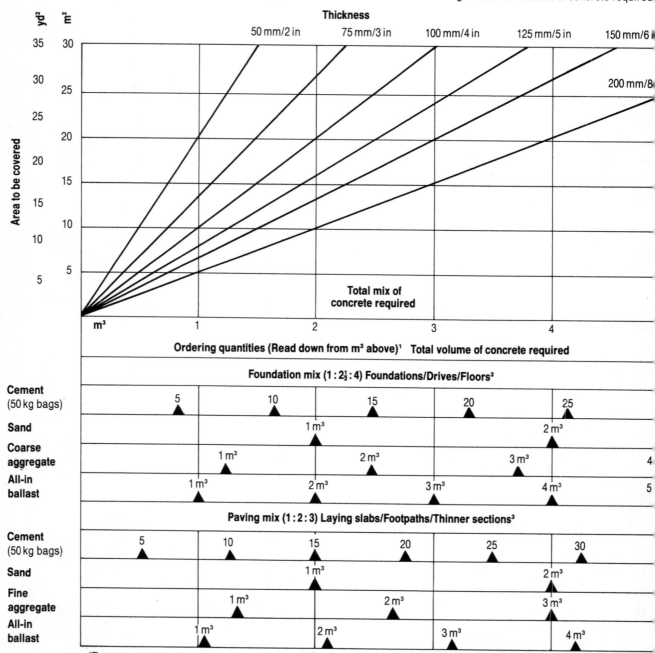

¹To convert cubic yards into cubic metres multiply by 0.7646.

²If using all-in ballast this mix becomes (1 : 5)
³If using all-in ballast this mix becomes (1 : 3.75)

Tools

Ordering quantities

If ordering Ready-mix concrete this will be your required amount but bear in mind that minimum orders are 3-4 m³. If ordering the separate constituents choose your mix and read off the different quantities required. The conventional way of describing a mix is in figures, i.e., (1:2:3). This always denotes the volume of cement first followed by the sand and finally the aggregate (stones).

Note. You can either buy sand and aggregate separately or use a combined ballast in which the sand is already mixed with the aggregate. Choose whichever is convenient or available and read off from that column. Round up the figures to the nearest ¼ m³ as this is the minimum measure that builders' merchants work to.

If only small amounts of concrete are required consider using dry-mix in bags. These contain everything you need, including the cement, are available in several mixes and carry full instructions on the bag. They are available in 25 and 50 kg bags.

Most of the tools required for occasional concreting can be found in the garden shed. Clean tools immediately after use, as dried cement is extremely difficult to remove.

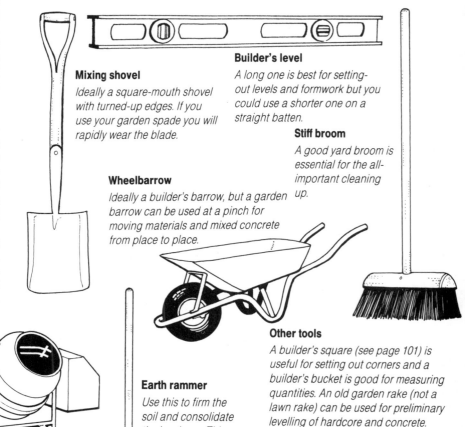

Mixing shovel

Ideally a square-mouth shovel with turned-up edges. If you use your garden spade you will rapidly wear the blade.

Wheelbarrow

Ideally a builder's barrow, but a garden barrow can be used at a pinch for moving materials and mixed concrete from place to place.

Builder's level

A long one is best for setting-out levels and formwork but you could use a shorter one on a straight batten.

Stiff broom

A good yard broom is essential for the all-important cleaning up.

Concrete mixer

Consider hiring a concrete mixer if you have large quantities to mix. Two-phase electric ones that work off the household supply are best. Clean it by putting some coarse aggregate and water in the barrel and leaving it to run for a while.

Earth rammer

Use this to firm the soil and consolidate the hardcore. This can make an important difference to the sub-base.

Other tools

A builder's square (see page 101) is useful for setting out corners and a builder's bucket is good for measuring quantities. An old garden rake (not a lawn rake) can be used for preliminary levelling of hardcore and concrete. A wide brush to dampen surfaces and a steel float for finishing, along with large polythene sheets to protect the concrete from drying out too quickly, completes the list.

Concrete and sub-base thicknesses

These recommended thicknesses will ensure that your concrete work will stand up to its intended use.

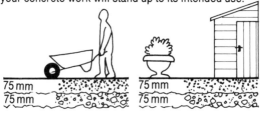

75 mm
75 mm

Garden paths

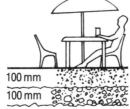

75 mm
75 mm

Sheds and summer houses

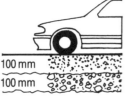

100 mm
100 mm

Patios and general purpose areas

100 mm
100 mm

Drives (Cars only)

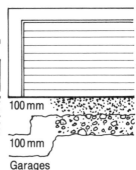

100 mm

100 mm

Garages (Increase to 200 mm beneath walls)

Bricks

It takes many years of training and experience to build a perfect brick wall but satisfying results can be achieved by the amateur on small garden walls with care and patience. Study a good book on the subject and learn with small unimportant jobs.

Brick sizes

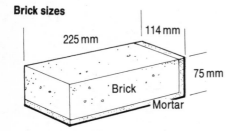

Brick module

Bricks are never made to an exact size and to overcome this problem a brick module has been devised. This includes mortar on two surfaces, so any variation is taken up by the mortar thickness to equal a standard area.

Estimating quantities

For the number of bricks required you should reckon on 58 per square metre or 48 per square yd. Always add 5 per cent to allow for wastage etc. If you have to go back to buy more the merchant may be out of stock and you could have a long wait to complete your project. A use can always be found for spare bricks if you have an excess.

Bricks are normally sold by the thousand but most stockists will happily sell smaller quantities.

Anatomy of a brick

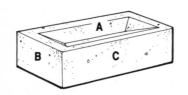

The indentation (**A**) on a brick is called a 'frog' and unless great strength is required lay bricks frog down. The short face is called the 'header' (**B**) and the long face the 'stretcher' (**C**). Half bricks are called bats and bricks split longitudinally are called queen closers.

Types of brick

Commons

The cheapest type of brick. Plain and uninteresting these are used where they will not be seen either covered by rendering or below ground level to save on cost.

Regrades

These are facing bricks that have failed to come up to standard and are therefore sold at less cost. Same usage as commons.

Facing bricks

These are designed to be seen and there's an enormous variety of shade, colour and texture to choose from. A good builders' merchant will have a brick library where you can ruminate at your leisure before choosing exactly what you want. You will probably have to wait some time for delivery from the manufacturer so plan ahead.

Hand-made bricks

The majority of bricks are machine-made but hand-made bricks are still available. They naturally cost more but they do make a far more interesting wall than machine-made bricks.

Second-hand bricks

Cleaned and selected second-hand bricks are now often more expensive than new ones due to an increased interest in mock-Georgian executive homes. However, if you see a house being demolished and you are prepared to clean (knock off the old mortar) yourself, it's worth making an offer to the site foreman—you may get a bargain.

Engineering bricks

Usually blue in colour, these are very hard frost-resistant bricks for special purposes but they are often used decoratively on garden walls.

Air brick

A specially made brick with holes through the face to allow ventilation under suspended floors etc.

Storing bricks

Bricks should be built into a loose stack with gaps at the bottom, to allow for ventilation, on a hard free-draining surface. Cover the top with heavy polythene sheeting to shed rain. If the weather has been very hot prior to use spray them lightly with a hose to reduce excessive suction from the mortar.

Mortar mixes

Mix A

For internal and external walls from damp-proof-course to eaves.

    1:5
Portland cement
Fine builders' sand
Add plasticizer*

Mix B

For freestanding walls, retaining walls and all brickwork below the damp-proof-course and below ground.

    1:4
Portland cement
Fine builders' sand
Add plasticizer*

*See manufacturer's instructions.

Plasticizers

Proprietary plasticizers using a mix of resins come in liquid form and are added to the water rather than the mix. They introduce air into the mortar to make it more pliable. They eliminate the need for lime in a mix and promote frost protection in new and hardened mortar.

Foundations

For freestanding walls dig a trench and level off a foundation concrete mix (see page 98). As a rough guide strip foundations can be sunk 700–800 mm (27–31 in) below ground level (**A**). Its thickness should equal the wall thickness (**B**) and its width should be twice the wall thickness (**C**). Protect retaining walls from the earth with a damp-proof-course (**D**) and protect the top with coping stones (**E**).

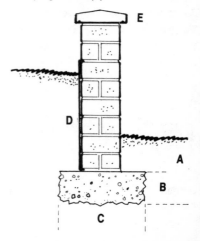

Tools

The tools described in Concreting (page 99) can be used to mix the mortar for bricklaying. In addition there are a few specialized tools required along with some general-purpose tools for satisfactory bricklaying.

Builder's level

You'll be using this a lot to check the horizontal and vertical placing of bricks so get a long one.

Pointing trowel

As its name suggests this is used for pointing between brick courses. The big trowel is too unwieldy for this.

Bricklayer's line and pins

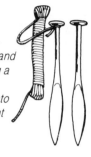

These provide a quick and easy guide when laying a line of bricks. The flat-ended end is pushed into a horizontal mortar joint along a length of wall with the line pulled taut between.

Bricklayer's trowel

Quality bricklayer's trowels have one straight and one curved edge to the blade and are either left or right-handed. The ones the DIYer is likely to acquire will be universal with both edges the same.

400 mm

500 mm

90°

300 mm

Builder's square

This is a very useful tool that you can make yourself. Construct it to the dimensions shown from planed softwood and check it against an accurate 90° angle. Screw and glue the joints so that it remains accurate. It's indispensable for setting out corners.

Gauge rod

This is another useful tool you can make yourself. Use a length of 50 × 25 mm (2 in × 1 in) planed softwood and measure 75 mm increments along its length. Mark these all round, using a try square, and make shallow saw cuts along each line. This can then be used to check the height of your brick courses as you build, in case your mortar thickness goes awry.

Spot board

Use a spot board—a piece of ply or chipboard about one metre square—supported on bricks to hold your mixed-up mortar conveniently close to hand.

Re-pointing a wall

You may find it necessary at some time to re-point a wall particularly in older buildings. If mortar is missing it allows the rain to soak into the brickwork. In the winter this freezes and cracks off part of the brick. This is known as spalling. If the job is not tackled it can eventually make structures unsafe. It's particularly galling with brick chimney stacks as they're too far away to notice. If the old mortar is soft—and it often is—and the affected area is not too large it's a relatively simple DIY job. If the mortar is hard you will need a plugging chisel and club hammer. Clean it out to a regular depth of 8–10 mm ($\frac{3}{8}$ in). Use mix **B**, opposite, for re-pointing.

When putting the final finish to joints do the vertical ones first and finish with the long horizontal joints.

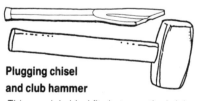
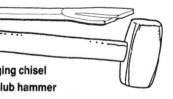

Plugging chisel and club hammer

This special chisel fits between the bricks and will remove old mortar neatly.

Joint rake

With hardwearing wheels and replaceable points this specially designed tool makes an odious job much easier.

Types of mortar joint

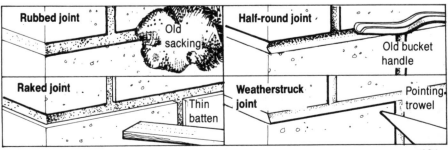

Rubbed joint — Old sacking

Half-round joint — Old bucket handle

Raked joint — Thin batten

Weatherstruck joint — Pointing trowel

Wall blocks

Concrete blocks for walling have been around for many years. Their appeal lies in the ease and speed with which a wall can be constructed as opposed to bricks—one block is equivalent to seven bricks—and their saving on cost.

They do require a surface finish to make them acceptable aesthetically, usually cement render outdoors and plaster inside. Manufactured from all sorts of waste materials, concrete blocks used to be heavy, difficult to cut and poor insulators. Most modern concrete blocks in use now are aerated and often made from pulverized fuel ash. They are light in both colour and weight, easy to cut and drill and nowadays are preferred for the inner leaf of cavity house walls, due to their superior insulating properties. They are an excellent alternative to hollow stud partition walls over solid floors in the house. The surface of these blocks is scored for improved adhesion to plaster.

Block walls can be built using the same tools and techniques as for bricklaying with a similar mortar mix (see page 100).

Sizes

Lightweight aerated blocks are available in a range of sizes the commonest being 450 × 215 mm (18 × 8½ in) and thicknesses of 100 mm (4 in), 125 mm (5 in) and 215 mm (8½ in). Visit your local stockist, measure the block you fancy and divide this into your proposed wall area. Add five per cent for wastage.

Control joints

Block walls move to a greater degree than their equivalent brick counterparts, so control joints need to be incorporated to take up this movement and avoid cracking. These should be made at 6 m (20 ft) intervals as well as around door and window openings and wall junctions. Rake the mortar from between the control joint when almost dry to a depth of about 19 mm (¾ in) and fill with a caulking compound.

Types of wall block
A. Dense concrete block

Made from heavy aggregates such as limestone, gravel and granite. These are heavy but very strong.

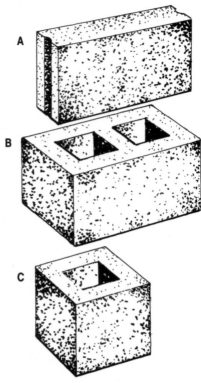

B. Cored concrete block

These can be used for building load-bearing internal walls.

C. Half-cored block

Used to stagger the joints in a wall built using **B**.

D. Lightweight aerated block

Thick lightweight block for load-bearing internal walls.

E. Lightweight aerated block

Thin lightweight block for inner leaves of cavity walls and non load-bearing internal walls.

F. Reconstituted stone facing block

An exterior wall block to replace brick. Has a decorative moulded surface to simulate real stone.

Wall ties

Wall ties are used to tie the two leaves of a cavity wall together as it is built up. Ties are incorporated in the brickwork and staggered at about six courses of brick vertically and four brick lengths horizontally.

A. Galvanized steel wall tie
A strong tie which has lost ground to the cheaper butterfly tie.

B. Butterfly wall tie
Inexpensive twisted wire wall tie.

C. Door frame tie
Galvanized steel tie for fixing to door frames when building in.

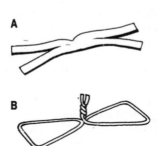

Screen blocks

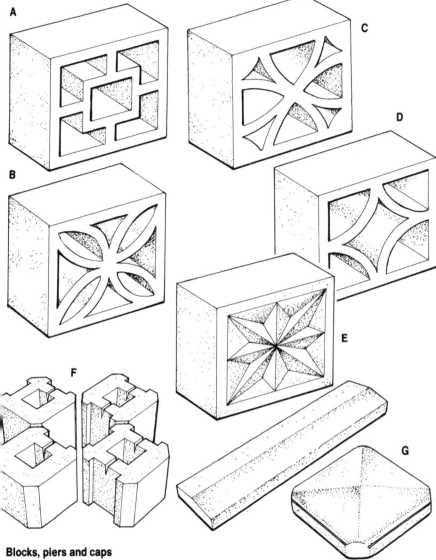

Screen blocks

Cast in white concrete, screen blocks make an attractive garden feature either to hide an unattractive view or give a certain amount of privacy without cutting out too much light. They look good as a backcloth to dark green plants and go particularly well incorporated with facing bricks in a low wall. Large areas can be rather overwhelming with the geometric design. They are inherently weak structures because they can only be stack-bonded, i.e., one block placed directly over another, and because of this they require careful building and reinforcing with piers.

Screen blocks are all of a standard size. $290 \times 290 \times 93$ mm ($11\frac{1}{2} \times 11\frac{1}{2} \times 3\frac{5}{8}$ in).

The special hollow blocks for building into piers are called pilasters and have slots to accept the blocks. Four types of pilaster are available: with one slot for finishing a wall, with two opposing slots for building into a straight wall, with two adjacent slots for turning a corner and with three slots for building another wall at right angles. Special pilaster caps complete the piers.

Foundations should be 200 mm (8 in) wider than the wall and, depending on your soil type, 75–100 mm (3–4 in) deep. Use the foundation mix on page 98. Piers should be incorporated at every 2.5–3 m (8–10 ft) and maximum recommended height is six courses.

Piers are further reinforced, unless the wall is low, with steel rods or angle-iron set into the foundation mortar while it is still wet. When the piers are built up, sloppy concrete is poured into the pilasters around the rods.

Mortar

For mortar use mix A on page 100. Be patient building with blocks as mortar stains will show on the white blocks. For a specially neat pointing use silver sand and white cement. Finish with a half-round joint (see page 101).

Note. Screen blocks cannot be cut so your wall must be a certain number of blocks long.

Take care when unloading and storing screen blocks as damage cannot be hidden. Some blocks have a moulding on the face, but this will be on one face only so plan accordingly.

Blocks, piers and caps

A. Square design block

Probably the most popular design for screen walling. A line of these go well set into a low brick wall.

B. Leaf block

Another design that looks well in a single line.

C. Maltese cross block

This makes an interesting pattern when built together.

D. Diamond block

Ideally this should be seen in fours as it then creates perfect circles.

E. North star block

This is a solid block with a pattern impressed into the face and is good for mixing with other designs to break up an otherwise repeating pattern.

F. Pilaster pier blocks

Hollow blocks with slots to locate in various configurations (see text, right).

G. Pilaster pier cap

For closing off the top of the pier.

H. Wall capping

Seals the top of the wall against rain.

Paving

Paving with slabs provides a way of covering large areas with impermeable material relatively quickly and with less complications than concrete. It is also more attractive, although it costs more.

However it is still very heavy work. Large slabs can weigh up to 60 kg (the weight of a small adult) and the site has to be prepared and thoroughly levelled with large amounts of base materials moved around.

It is satisfying work though, because transformation from plan to completion is almost instant.

The key to perfect paving, like most things, is in the preparation. If the site is not properly prepared, slabs will start to rock and may even crack, necessitating further work at a later date.

Manufactured slabs

There are basically two types of manufactured slab: hydraulically pressed slabs are about 38 mm (1½ in) thick and are strong enough to support the weight of a car—albeit with the proper foundations—and, vibrated concrete slabs which are thicker but crack more easily and should only be used for pedestrian areas.

Sizes

There are so many varying shapes and sizes it would be difficult to list them here. Visit garden centres and builders' merchants, armed with an expanding rule and a note-pad, and take the dimensions of those which take your fancy. You can then plan your design at home on graph paper to give you the exact number required.

Tools

The tools required for slab-laying are basically those shown for concreting (page 99).

Paving slab shapes

A. Large square slab

Will cover large areas quickly but is heavy to manoeuvre.

B. Long narrow slab

Creates a more interesting pattern than square slabs.

C. Hexagonal slab

An interesting design but can pose problems on corners.

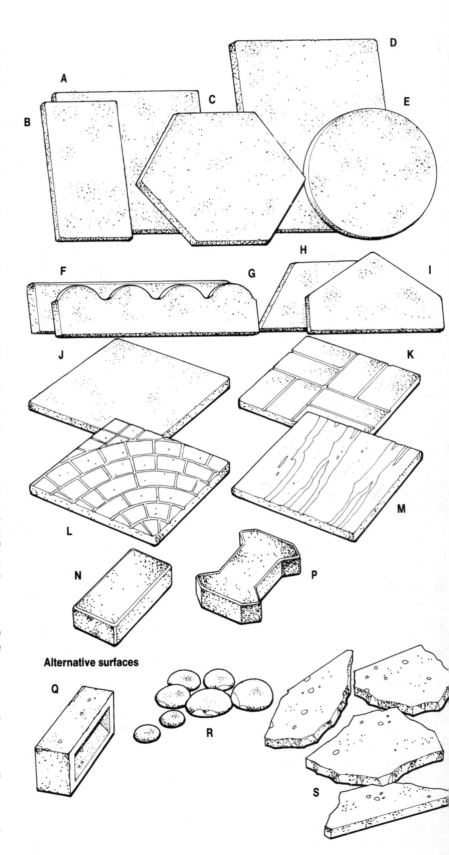

Alternative surfaces

Paving

D. Large rectangular slab

E. Circular slab

An unusual design which needs careful planning and laying. The spaces need to be filled with an alternative material—gravel perhaps? These make good stepping-stones set in a lawn.

F & G. Edging stones

Two types of edging stones which are used in conjunction with path materials like gravel.

H & I. Half hexagons

Used to provide a straight edge to **C** (above).

Textured slabs

J. Smooth slab

This is the basic slab finish but most incorporate some kind of anti-slip sanded surface.

K. Impressed brick

This looks like bricks laid in alternate pairs.

L. Impressed cobbles

This is meant to simulate the way cobbles were laid. Can be laid in sets of four to create large circles.

M. Riven finish

The nearest look that you'll get to natural stone. This copies the attractive split finish of natural quarried stone.

N & P. Paving bricks

Becoming very popular but should really be laid professionally as the sub-base needs to be levelled very carefully and compacted using special equipment.

Q. Brick

If you have a quantity of old bricks they can make a very attractive path or paved area, but they do tend to crumble when frost gets at them.

R. Cobbles

Garden centres sell large pebbles for setting in concrete, but they should only be used as architectural features as they are uncomfortable to walk on.

S. Crazy paving

Usually obtained cheaply from local authorities as broken pavement slabs. This old surface treatment still looks very attractive.

Important

Any base construction that does not include a damp-proof-course and abuts the house wall must be at least 150 mm (6 in) below the house DPC.

A fall away from the house wall of 25 mm in every 3 m (1 in in 10 ft) is required to shed rainwater and avoid puddles forming.

Set paving below the level of the lawn so that the mower runs cleanly over the edge.

There are two methods of laying slabs: direct on to levelled and compacted sharp sand or, dabs of mortar (five per large slab) on to the same type of base.

Cutting slabs

Measure and mark off a line parallel to the edge using a straight batten. If the slab is light coloured, use a soft pencil and if dark, scratch the surface using an old screwdriver. Lay the slab on a level bed of sand and tap along the line using a wide bolster chisel and club hammer. Turn the slab over and continue on the other side. Repeat this until the sound of the blows change, indicating that the slab is cracking. It's possible to get quite an accurate cut with this method, but some dense materials like smooth coping stones will not crack cleanly. Borrow or hire an angle-grinder with a carborundum disc (see page 49) and use this instead.

Bases for paving

Slab or block
House wall
Fall
25 mm per 3 m
(1 in per 10 ft)
A
B
Firm soil
Min.
150 mm DPC
(6 in)

Recommended thicknesses

Paths A. 25 – 38 mm (1–1½ in)
  B. 50 mm (2 in)
Patios A. 38–50 mm (1½–2 in)
  B. 75–100 mm (3–4 in)

Drives A. 60–75 mm (2½–3 in)
  B. 100–150 mm (4–6 in)

A. – Levelled and compacted sharp sand.
B. – Well rammed hardcore.

Gravel

Undoubtedly, a gravel drive has an air of gracious living about it, but it must be contained and never allowed to creep under wooden garage doors or boarded gates, as it will tear splinters off the bottom and allow rot to set in.

It also requires a well made sub-base to avoid being churned up.

Base construction for drives and edge restraints for paths and drives.

13 mm (½ in) washed pea shingle
25 mm (1 in) hoggin*
50 mm (2 in) coarse gravel
100 mm (4 in) hardcore
*Fine gravel mixed with clay

Treated wooden board
fixed to stake

Edging stone
set in concrete

Fences

Fences are something that almost any homeowner will have to replace at some time or other. They are often neglected and after the first gales of winter they suffer the consequences. Fences are afflicted by two problems; being made of wood, they rot, and they present a very high resistance to wind. Every January one can see the result. To prevent rot in fences—and particularly to wooden posts—they should be treated about every three years with either creosote (cheap) or wood preservative (more expensive). See page 16.

Sometimes a post can be saved by cutting off the bottom and fitting it into a special metal socket which is then set in concrete (see right).

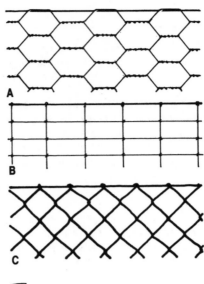

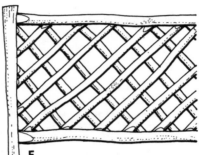

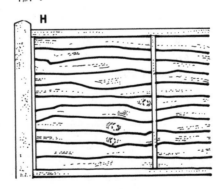

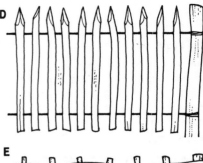

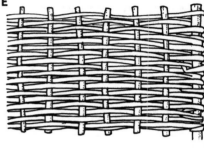

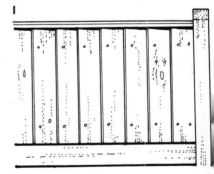

Types of fencing

A. Galvanized wire netting

An extremely basic form of boundary enclosure, this can only be considered a temporary measure.

Sizes: in continuous rolls of 10 m (33 ft) and heights of 600 mm (2 ft) and 900 mm (3 ft).

B. Woven wire fencing

Stretched between posts, this is mainly for livestock, so you will probably only find it at agricultural suppliers.

C. Chain-link fencing

This is PVC-coated galvanized wire and is only marginally better than A.

Sizes: this is available in a large range of sizes for industrial users, but is normally found in 10 m (33 ft) rolls by 900 m (3 ft) and 1200 mm (4 ft).

D. Chestnut paling

Simple, rustic boundary fence.

Size: 9 m (10 yd) rolls by 900 mm (3 ft), 1100 mm (3½ ft), 1200 mm (4 ft) and 1370 mm (4½ ft).

E. Wattle hurdles

These make an attractive small fence and are usually found in a garden where a hedge is growing.

Size: 2 m (6 ft) long by 600 mm (2 ft) to 900 mm (3 ft) high.

F. Rustic wood

These are made from branches rather than sawn timber and fit well into decorative planting schemes.

Sizes: Almost any size can be made to order.

G. Picket fence

You can construct this yourself or find a local supplier.

H. Interwoven fence panels

These are designed to drop between slot-ted concrete posts. They are rather fragile but are the cheapest way of getting a peep-proof fence.

Sizes: 2 m (6 ft) long by 900 mm (3 ft), 1200 mm (4 ft), 1500 mm (5 ft) and 1800 mm (6 ft).

I. Closeboard fence

This is probably the strongest wooden fence that you can get. It has either oak or concrete posts and the boards can either be set closely side by side or overlapped, in which case they are feather-edge boards.

Gates

Parts of a fence

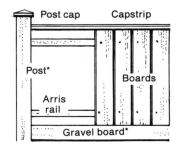

*Either timber or concrete

Fence repair accessories

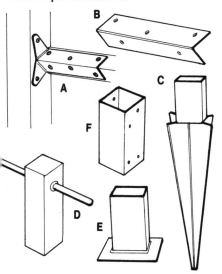

A. Arris rail repair bracket

If the tenon of a rail breaks, this galvanized bracket can be screwed to the rail and wooden post

B. Arris rail angle bracket

Repairs the rail if broken elsewhere.

C. Metal post support

Can be used to replace the lower rotten portion of a wooden post. Available for 75 mm (3 in) posts and 50 mm (2 in) posts.

D. Metal dolly

For driving post supports into the ground.

E. Metal base

For concreting-in wooden posts.

F. Post extender

For extending 75 mm (3 in) wooden posts.

Entrance gates

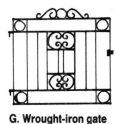

G. Wrought-iron gate

H. Simple wooden gate

I. Heavy drive gate

There are numerous designs of gate and a tour around all the local outlets should turn up something to your liking. Also check the Yellow Pages for local craftsmen who will build to order. Alternatively, if you're good at joinery, design and build your own. Whatever type you choose, it puts gate posts under great strain so make sure they are not rotted where they enter the soil.

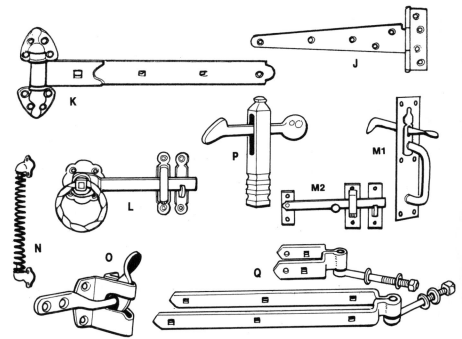

Gate hardware

J. Light strap hinge

Suitable for light-boarded side gates.

K. Heavy steel strap hinge

Suitable for drive gates.

L. Ring latch

Decorative latch for entrance gates.

M. Suffolk latch

M1 shows external part. M2 shows internal side (not to scale). Use on close-boarded side gates with J.

N. Coil gate spring

Closes gates automatically. Works well with O.

O. Automatic latch

Secures with a push of the gate. Useful when you've got your hands full.

P. Gate stop

Set into concrete, this holds the gate open until released.

Q. Double strap hinge

Suitable for heavy drive gates. The bolt passes through the gatepost.

Emergencies!

Use this table as a quick guide for when emergencies arise. Precious moments can be saved if you acquaint yourself with the locations of important items like electricity consumer units, where your fuses or circuit-breakers are housed, your water supply stopcock, hot water system stopcocks or stop-valves and your main gas tap.

Problem	Possible Cause	Check	Action
ELECTRICITY Sudden loss of all power.	Power cut.	Look outside to see if nearby houses are totally dark (at night) or ask neighbours (daytime).	Organize emergency lighting—torches, lanterns and candles. Wait for power to come back on. Check that any electric fires are switched off if you go to bed before power is restored.
One circuit only out, i.e., power or lighting.	Fuse at consumer unit. MCB tripped. Faulty wiring/appliance.	Switch off mains supply. Check consumer unit for blown fuses or MCBs for tripping.	Assess reason for blown fuse. Renew fuse—reset MCB. If fuse blows repeatedly, call electrician.
Bang at socket. Appliance not working.	Plug fuse blown. Plug wiring faulty.	Check plug fuse. Check plug wiring.	Replace fuse of correct rating (see page 50). Re-wire plug (see page 50).
Acrid burning smell.	Faulty wiring on plug, appliance or socket.	Appliance or plug wiring.	Re-wire or call electrician.
Single light not working.	Faulty or blown bulb. Faulty wiring.	Bulb. Wiring at switch or lampholder.	Replace (see page 56). Turn off supply and re-wire or call electrician.
WATER No water at all.	Water turned off (Water Board should have notified you). Damaged pipe.	Are men working outside digging up the road (Water Board vehicles)? Are other contractors (builders) working nearby?	Wait for supply to come back on. Call the Water Board.
Poor flow and/or sediment in mains water supply.	Damaged or leaking mains pipe.		Call the Water Board.
COLD WATER SUPPLY cold water system leaking.	Frozen pipe (now thawed out after cold spell). Damaged pipe. Loose pipe connections.	Find where leak is occurring.	Locate the stopcock and turn off (see page 58). Open all cold taps and flush toilets. Don't use any hot water. Arrange containers to catch leaks. Call plumber.
HOT WATER SYSTEM Water dripping through ceiling (not raining).	Corroded cold water tank leaking. Damaged pipe in loft.	Go into loft to find cause.	Turn off stop-valve to cold water tank—if there is one—or tie up the ball-valve (see right). Open all hot taps starting with those located highest in the house. Note: if the leak is definitely in the hot water system you can still use the cold water supply. Switch off all boilers and water heaters and put out any boiler fire. Call plumber.

Emergencies!

Problem	Possible Cause	Check	Action
Other leaks from hot water system.	Faulty fittings. Faulty pipes. Leaking hot water cylinder.	Find source of leak.	As left. It may be necessary to drain the hot water cylinder.
GAS Strong smell of gas in the street.	Fractured gas main.		Warn others. Call the Gas Board immediately.
Strong smell of gas in the home.	Faulty appliance. Gas left on unlit. Pilot lights blown out.		Turn off supply. Open all windows and doors. Do not operate light switches. Wait for smell to disperse and if it does not call the Gas Board.
Boilers or fires burning very erratically.	Damaged gas main.		Call the Gas Board.

Note. Even though the electricity may be cut off most telephones will still work—they have their own supply.

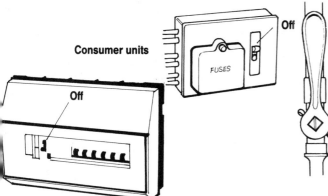

Consumer units

Off

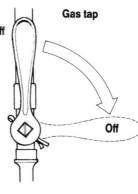

Gas tap

Off

Off

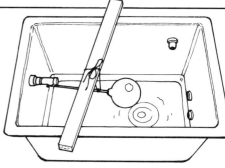

Tying up a ball-valve

Place a batten across the tank top, wind string around the ballcock arm and tie securely to the batten.

Emergency telephone numbers

ELECTRICITY	GAS	WATER
ELECTRICIAN (List at least two)	**PLUMBER** (List at least two)	

Index

Conversion tables

Comparison of millimetres and inches

METRIC — Centimetres and millimetres

IMPERIAL — Inches and fractions

Conversion factors

To convert *to* metric, multiply by the factor shown.
To convert *from* metric, divide by the factor shown.

Length

Miles – kilometres	1.6093
Yards – metres	0.9144
Feet – metres	0.3048
Inches – millimetres	25.4
Inches – centimetres	2.54

Area

Acres – square metres	4046.86
Square yards – square metres	0.8361
Square feet – square metres	0.0929
Square inches – square millimetres	645.16

Volume

Cubic yards – cubic metres	0.7646
Cubic feet – cubic metres	0.0283
Cubic inches – cubic centimetres	16.3871

Capacity

Gallons – litres	4.546
Quarts – litres	1.137
Pints – litres	0.568

Velocity

Miles per hour – kilometres per hour	1.6093
Feet per second – metres per second	0.3048

Mass

Tons – tonnes	1.0160
Hundredweights – kilograms	50.8023
Stones – kilograms	6.3503
Pounds – kilograms	0.4536
Ounces – grams	28.3495

Fuel consumption

Gallons per mile – litres per kilometre	2.825
Miles per gallon – kilometres per litre	0.354

Temperature

Fahrenheit	Celsius
230°	110°
220°	
210°	100°
200°	90°
190°	
180°	80°
170°	
160°	70°
150°	
140°	60°
130°	50°
120°	
110°	
100°	40°
90°	
80°	30°
70°	
60°	20°
50°	10°
40°	
30°	0°
20°	
10°	−10°
0°	−20°

Boiling point of water 212°F — Boiling point of water 100°C

Freezing point of water 32°F — Freezing point of water 0°C

International paper sizes

Size	mm	Inches
A0	841 × 1189	33.11 × 46.81
A1	594 × 841	23.39 × 33.11
A2	420 × 594	16.54 × 23.39
A3	297 × 420	11.69 × 16.54
A4	210 × 297	8.27 × 11.69
A5	148 × 210	5.83 × 8.27

Abbreviations

Centilitre	cl	metre	m
Centimetre	cm	Milligram	mg
Cubic centimetre	cm³	Millilitre	ml
Cubic metre	m³	Millimetre	mm
Cubic millimetre	mm³	Minute	min
Foot	ft	Ounce	oz
Gallon	gal	Pint	pt
Gram	g	Pound	lb
Hour	h	Quart	qt
Hundredweight	cwt	Square centimetre	cm²
Inch	in	Square kilometre	km²
Kilogram	kg	Square metre	m²
Kilometre	km	Square mile	sq mile
Litre	l	Square millimetre	mm²
		Yard	yd